RAILROADS IN THE DAYS OF STEAM

ILLUSTRATED WITH PAINTINGS, PRINTS, DRAWINGS
AND PHOTOGRAPHS OF THE PERIOD

RAILROADS

Published by

AMERICAN HERITAGE PUBLISHING CO., INC., NEW YORK

Book Trade Distribution by GOLDEN PRESS · NEW YORK

IN THE DAYS OF STEAM

by the editors of AMERICAN HERITAGE

The Magazine of History

narrative by ALBERT L. McCREADY

in consultation with LAWRENCE W. SAGLE

Curator, Baltimore and Ohio Transportation Museum, Baltimore, Maryland

FOREWORD

THE STORY of America's railroads is truly the story of the growth and development of America itself. Fascinating in all its aspects, this story graphically illustrates the westering spirit that dominated our forebears, and carried them across the continent.

Following the birth of the railroad in Baltimore, in 1827, lines spread west, north, and south, spinning a magic web of steel rails which bound the country together, and made it the great industrial giant that it is today.

Nothing has ever seemed to equal the fascination of the days when a little eight-wheeler could be seen belching smoke as it clanked along, dragging a train of wooden freight cars or shiny yellow passenger coaches behind it. Those early years were filled with romance: the thrill of Promontory Point; Indian raids; train robberies; the conquering of high mountain ranges; and the long, long trek across the wide prairies.

During the Civil War, the importance of the railroad for the movement of troops and supplies was immediately recognized by the armies of both the North and South. For such military purposes, the railroads have never been surpassed, as two world wars have demonstrated.

Railroading men—such as Winans, Baldwin, Janney, Westinghouse, and Pullman, to name a few—have worked with unselfish devotion to improve the safety and operation of the railroads as well as to insure the comforts of passengers. From the day when Evans trundled his little steam scow through the streets of Philadelphia, to the swift-running diesel-powered, strata-domed streamliners of today, men have worked untiringly to make our railroads the finest in the world.

In the following pages, the author, Albert L. McCready, has gathered together some of the most fascinating moments in American railroading history. His narrative, illustrated as it is with a wealth of contemporary paintings, prints, and photographs, will bring young readers a vital understanding of the adventure and romance which attended the building and development of America's railroads.

LAWRENCE W. SAGLE

LIBRARY OF CONGRESS CATALOGUE CARD NUMBER: 60–8812

© 1960 by American Heritage Publishing Co., Inc. All rights reserved under Berne and Pan-American Copyright Conventions. Reproduction in whole or in part in any form, without permission, is prohibited. Designed by Artists and Writers Press, Inc. Printed in the U. S. A. by Western Printing and Lithographing Company. Published by American Heritage Publishing Co., Inc., 551 Fifth Avenue, New York 17, N. Y.

Tramway lines, with cars drawn by horses or men, made hauling easier at factories and in mines in eighteenth-century England. This drawing shows a cart at the coal mines at Newcastle in 1773.

CONTENTS

Most American roads were still rough and primitive when Latrobe's watercolor was painted early in the 1800's. This scene shows a farmer with an oxcart.

THE COMING OF STEAM

For a hundred years after the Pilgrim Fathers landed at Plymouth Rock in 1620, there were almost no roads in America. People found it much faster and more comfortable to travel to coastal cities by ship. Visitors to the backwoods learned that it was easier to paddle canoes up the rivers than to follow Indian trails through the forests.

As the colonies grew, roads improved, but in 1756, it still took covered wagons three days to make the ninety-mile trip between New York and Philadelphia.

Settlements had been made on the other side of the Allegheny Mountains in eastern New York and Pennsylvania. But since mountain trails could not be used by wheeled vehicles, supplies for the settlers had to be carried on pack horses.

Even before the Revolution, there was much talk of the need for roads across the mountain barrier. The rivers on the western slopes flowed into the Ohio River. The Ohio, in turn, emptied into the mighty Mississippi, which flowed south to New Orleans. The people of the Atlantic seaboard wanted to bring western trade into cities on the east coast.

The stone-paved Lancaster Pike, built in 1794, ran sixty-two miles west of Lancaster, Pennsylvania. It was the first good wagon road leading toward the Ohio Valley. Twenty years later, the federal-built Cumberland Road (also known as the National Pike) was begun. It eventually reached St. Louis, Missouri.

By 1810 coastal roads were better, but the inland movement of freight by horses and wagons remained slow and expensive. Water transportation was still quicker and cheaper. Several states, and a few private companies, began to discuss removing snags and sand bars from the

Orukter Amphibolos, a steam dredge, was built by Oliver Evans in 1804.

rivers. Barge canals were dug into the foothills of the Alleghenies.

The Erie Canal, which cost over seven million dollars and took eight years to build, began service in October, 1825.

"The Big Ditch," as the canal was called, was four feet deep and forty

The busy new Erie Canal was painted by a schoolgirl artist in 1832.

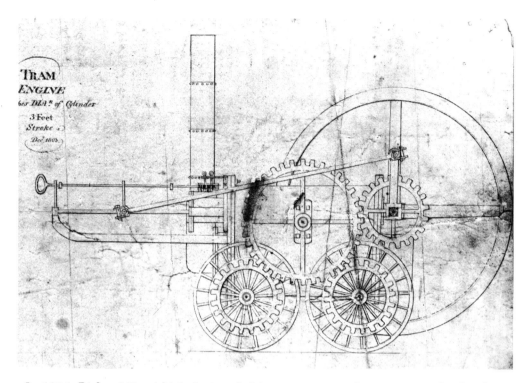

In 1804, Richard Trevithick designed this steam-powered tram engine for hauling carts of ore in an English iron mine. Up until then, horses had hauled the ore.

feet wide. It connected Albany on the Hudson River with Buffalo on Lake Erie. Wagons had taken twenty days to go from Albany to Buffalo. But canalboats could make the trip in five days. Freight rates dropped from $100 to $5 a ton.

In New York City, lower freight rates meant lower prices. New York became a flourishing trade center. When other eastern cities saw how much New York owed to the Erie Canal, they soon began to want to build canals, too. But steep mountains, where canals could not be built, barred Baltimore, Boston, and Philadelphia from the west. So New York's rival cities tried to solve their problems by turning to an Eng-

lishman named James Watt, and his strange invention, the steam engine.

Britain had threatened a penalty of a year's imprisonment and a fine of 200 pounds sterling for anyone informing Americans of Watt's machine, but somehow the news was smuggled across the Atlantic.

One of the first Americans to realize the value of the steam engine was the inventor, Oliver Evans.

One day in 1804, the people of Philadelphia blinked in astonishment as the doors of Evans' workshop opened. Out waddled his new steam dredge—a strange monster, puffing great clouds of smoke and sparks. It was a combination wagon and boat, with a steam engine hooked both to its wheels and to a paddle on the rear. It lumbered noisily down the cobblestone street to the Schuylkill River and plunged right in. *Orukter Amphibolos*, as it was called, was the first steam-powered vehicle in America, and the world's first amphibious steam engine.

In 1813, Evans outlined a plan for building a steam carriage-way between New York and Philadelphia. He said he could build a steam wagon and run it on wooden rails. He thought such a vehicle could speed along at fifteen miles an hour.

Evans was called a crackpot, but he did not lose confidence. Shortly before he died in 1819, he said:

"I do verily believe that carriages propelled by steam will come into general use, and travel at the rate of 300 miles a day."

The builder of the world's first successful railway locomotive was

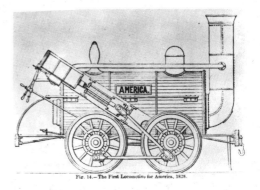

Fig. 14.—The First Locomotive for America, 1828.

In England, the locomotive America *was built for George Stephenson in 1828.*

an Englishman named Richard Trevithick—a Cornwall mine operator. He was familiar with the tramways and steam engines. He thought the two could be combined.

Trevithick built a steam engine with a heavy flywheel and geared it to the wheels of a flat car. In 1804, his locomotive hooked onto a load of nine tons of iron ore on a tramway serving a dock in South Wales. The track was poor and sometimes the

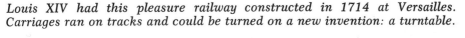

Louis XIV had this pleasure railway constructed in 1714 at Versailles. Carriages ran on tracks and could be turned on a new invention: a turntable.

little engine's wheels slipped. But it kept puffing along at five miles an hour until it had delivered its load to the Pennydarran Iron Works at Merthyr Tydfil, nine miles inland.

Only one more idea was now needed to give the world its first real railroad: the locomotive must be put to public use. This remained for the great English inventor, George Stephenson, to do.

He was an employee of the Stockton & Darlington Railway, which received a charter from the Crown in 1821 to operate a public tramway in North Ireland "for hauling of wagons and other carriages . . . with men or horses or otherwise."

Young Stephenson told the directors of the new railway that the word "otherwise" entitled them to use a steam locomotive to pull their trains, and that he could build one. On September 27, 1825, the *Locomotion No. 1* was ready for its trial trip.

An eyewitness set down this description of the Stockton & Darlington train on the historic day. It was made up of: "The *Locomotion*, driven by George Stephenson. Tender with water and coals. Six wagons, loaded with coals, passengers on top

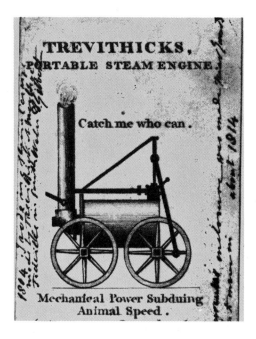

This English railway ticket shows Trevithick's engine, the Catch Me Who Can.

A Stephenson engine runs on England's Liverpool & Manchester line in 1830.

This would seem a very long and heavy train for an untried locomotive. But the total weight of Stephenson's engine, and the thirty cars trailing behind it probably totaled only eighty tons, or about as much as one of today's Pullman cars.

After subtracting the time lost through a couple of derailments, the railroad's owners figured that the *Locomotion No. 1* and its train had averaged a speed of eight miles an hour for the trip. They were so pleased that they gave the unused coals to the poor, and "victuals and ale" to their workmen.

But it was a joyous occasion for an even greater reason—the era of steam railroading had arrived.

of them. One wagon, loaded with sacks of flour, passengers among them. One wagon containing the surveyor and engineers. Coach occupied by the director and proprietors. Six wagons filled with strangers. Fourteen wagons packed with workmen and others."

Locomotion No. 1, *driven by Stephenson, on its first passenger run in 1827.*

Tom Thumb, built by Peter Cooper in 1830, draws a pair of fancy cars.

THE IRON HORSE

Steel locomotives were pulling trains of cars along three common carrier railroads in England by 1830. But the United States was still gripped by "canal fever." By 1825, at least nineteen canals other than the Erie were in use, or were being dug. Canal barges were so popular that few Americans believed the railroads would ever rival them. In fact, the first steam engine to run on commercial railway tracks in America was built for a canal company.

The directors of the Delaware & Hudson Canal Company operated a 108-mile canal connecting the Delaware River at Honesdale, Pennsylvania, to the Hudson River at Ron-

dout, New York. Their company also owned a 16-mile horse railway used to bring coal to Honesdale from the mines at Carbondale, Pennsylvania.

Hearing of the successful use of steam locomotives on coal tramways in England, the company sent its young chief engineer, Horatio Allen, to look into the matter. He returned with four engines, the *Delaware,* the *Hudson,* the *America,* and the *Stourbridge Lion,* built for him there at a total cost of $12,515.58.

On August 8, 1829, Allen took the *Lion* on its first and only trip on the Carbondale-Honesdale railway. Its seven-ton bulk was thought to be too much for a bridge across Lackawax-

en Creek, built to support only three tons. Allen's friends tried to stop him from running the heavy engine over it. A Pennsylvania newspaper reported that Horatio Allen crossed "the trembling trestle" at a speed of "ten miles an hour amid deafening cheers."

Horatio Allen took a new job with a railroad in South Carolina, which had been trying, with small success, to propel its cars with sails. This railroad was built by the merchants of the city of Charleston, South Carolina. Their leadership in the cotton trade was being challenged by the city of Savannah, Georgia.

To answer this threat to the growth of their city, Charleston merchants organized in 1827 the South

The sailcar (above left) tested on the South Carolina Railroad, and the horse treadmill car (above) tried out on the Charleston & Hamburg, soon gave way to steam-powered locomotives such as the Stourbridge Lion *(below).*

In 1830 the Tom Thumb *ran a race with a horse-drawn tram—and the horse won.*

Carolina Canal & Railroad Company—the name showing that they were not sure whether a railway or a waterway was needed. By 1830, they had decided to build a 137-mile railroad, to run from Charleston to Hamburg, opposite Augusta, Georgia, on the Savannah River.

Soon after Horatio Allen went on the payroll, the company placed an order with the West Point Foundry in New York for a steam locomotive. It arrived on a coastal packet in October, 1830, to receive a civic welcome and the hopeful name of *Best Friend of Charleston.*

In its first tests, the *Best Friend* proved able to step along by itself at 30 to 35 miles an hour. It could pull loads of as many as fifty passengers, in a half-dozen cars, at 21 miles an hour. On Christmas Day it

went into regular service—the first American-built steam locomotive to haul a train of passenger cars on a public railroad.

Six months later, the *Best Friend* scored another first in United States railroading history when its boiler exploded. This accident has been blamed on a fireman who did not like the noise made by steam hissing through the safety valve. While the engine was standing at the end of the line, he sat on the safety valve lever. For a few moments there was peaceful silence. Then the *Best Friend of Charleston* blew up, scattering pieces of itself over the South Carolina landscape. The fireman died of his injuries.

Early railway coaches were designed in the same style as stagecoaches; they had no center aisle. The graceful coach (at right) is the Comet, *built by Ross Winans.*

18

Railroads had their bitter enemies in this period. Owners of canal companies and stagecoach lines were afraid that the iron horse would put them out of business. Some of these men spread the story of the South Carolina accident. In taverns and town halls, railroad-haters told bloodcurdling tales of steam locomotives. If they did not blow up with a fearful loss of life and limb, they would frighten horses and cause runaways—or the sparks from their smokestacks would set fire to crops and forests.

These were strong arguments. As a result, the builders of railroads in some areas found people anything but friendly. Surveying crews often were chased out of the fields by angry farmers with pitchforks.

Yet the railroads kept on building. The Baltimore & Ohio was chartered in 1827 at the urging of Baltimore

The Winchester *(right) built in 1832 was little more than three stagecoach bodies, run together, and set on a pair of swivelling four-wheel trucks: another of Winans' inventions.*

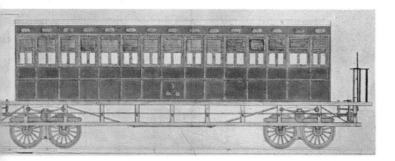

The center-aisle plan of construction used in Winans' Washington (left) set a new American standard.

Peter Cooper (left) invented the Tom Thumb, *a tiny, powerful steam engine.*

merchants. They were worried about their trade future now that the Erie Canal was bringing the bulk of western trade to New York.

They dreamed of the day when B & O tracks would extend into the heart of the Ohio Valley.

By 1830, the people of Baltimore were having doubts about the future of their railroad. Only thirteen miles of track had been built, at great expense, and trains were still horse-drawn. George Stephenson, the pioneer British locomotive builder, had said that no steam engine could be made to go around the sharp curves on the B & O line. Peter Cooper, a New York inventor and manufacturer who had bought land in Baltimore at the height of the enthusiasm for the B & O, thought differently. He told railroad officials that he could build a steam locomotive which would stay on the curving, twisting rails.

The one-horsepower *Tom Thumb* which Cooper built weighed no more than a ton, and looked like a toy. B & O horsecar drivers laughed when they saw it. Even the B & O directors were doubtful when they climbed into a boat-shaped car for the trial run of their new engine on August 25, 1830.

But the *Tom Thumb* was surprisingly strong, despite its dinky size. In 45 minutes it chugged along seven miles of track to Relay, the midway point where horses were changed on B & O cars bound for

The West Point's *barrier car of cotton bales protected riders from boiler explosions.*

When its boiler exploded, the Best Friend of Charleston's *fireman was killed.*

the end of the line at Ellicott's Mills. When the little engine arrived at the Mills, still puffing along as sturdily as ever, the directors were very pleased. When the *Tom Thumb* reached Relay on its return trip to Baltimore, there on a parallel track stood a horsecar with a grinning driver, eager to prove that he could outrace the "teakettle on a truck."

As soon as the *Tom Thumb* went by, the driver whipped up his horse, and the race was on. The horsecar quickly drew ahead, but Cooper threw another armload of pine knots on the fire and the little engine, with black smoke and sparks belching from its stack, speeded up and soon passed the galloping horse. Then a belt slipped, steam pressure dropped, and the *Tom Thumb* fell behind. The horse won the seven-mile race

from Relay to Baltimore. But officials had seen what steam power could do, and decided to build more locomotives. As a result, the B & O today is the oldest American railroad in continuous existence.

News of the success of the first steam trains in Baltimore and Charleston traveled swiftly. By 1835, three railroad lines were fanning out from Boston.

Thirteen railways were chartered by the New York legislature between 1826 and 1831. Work began

Robert Stevens (right) invented the T-rail in 1831. The T-rail, which quickly replaced early wooden rails topped with strap iron, is still in use. Its familiar shape is that seen in today's steel rails.

21

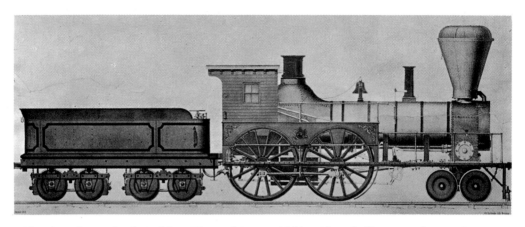

The Amoskeag, *built in New Hampshire in 1851 with a balloon smoke stack, was soberly decorated in comparison with other early locomotives of the steam age.*

in 1835 on the New York & Erie, and on the Mohawk & Hudson. Chartered in 1826 to build tracks between Albany and Schenectady, the M & H was the original line in today's New York Central System.

In Pennsylvania, too, the opening of the Erie Canal had been regarded as a calamity. Philadelphia merchants knew it would hurt their city, which was then the commercial and banking center of the nation. In 1828, the Pennsylvania legislature ordered the building of the Main Line of Public Works, a system of canals and railways linking Philadelphia with the Ohio River.

The first step was a double-tracked, horse-drawn railway from Philadelphia to Columbia. There,

The New Jersey, *built in Patterson, was decorated in front and on its cab with gingerbread filigree similar to that found on the great Mississippi steamboats.*

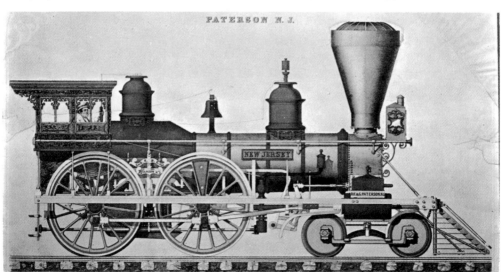

The Wyoming, *built in Philadelphia in 1857, was one of the gaudiest engines of its day, with surfaces covered with brightly painted scrollwork and flashing brass.*

freight and passengers were transferred to canalboats for the ride up the Susquehanna and Juniata rivers to the base of the Alleghenies.

Now came the really remarkable portion of the Main Line. Canalboats were lifted from the water and placed on flatcars. Then they were hauled, first by horses and later by steam, up a series of five more inclined planes. Each of these was a half mile long and lifted the boats two hundred feet.

A canalboat named the *Hit or Miss* was the first to make the complete trip over the Alleghenies in this unlikely fashion in 1835. Rolling down the western slope of the

The Lawrence, *built in Massachusetts at the Lawrence Manufacturing Company in 1853, had a large diamond stack, enamel panels on its cab, and bright metalwork.*

mountains on another series of inclined railways, it plunked into the Ohio River and drifted downstream to St. Louis.

But the Pennsylvania state transportation system could not compete with the Erie Canal. It was too slow and too expensive to operate.

Pennsylvania legislators studied their maps, and noted that a railroad built right across their state would offer a shorter route to Ohio, Indiana, and Illinois than those followed by the New York & Erie or the Baltimore & Ohio railroads. In 1846 the legislature created the new Pennsylvania Railroad Company, with a charter to build a 249-mile line across the Alleghenies to Pittsburgh.

In 1852 a famous figure in early-day railroading, John Edgar Thom-son, became president of the Pennsylvania Company. He startled directors by suggesting the railroad should invest in other companies building tracks in Ohio and Indiana. Some thought this a foolish idea, since the Pennsylvania still had an expensive tracklaying job of its own to pay for. But Thomson said his plan would shape the routes of these western lines so they would connect with Pennsylvania tracks at Pittsburgh. And it would also help build up the western states so there would be more freight for the Pennsy to haul. Following this policy, the Pennsylvania expanded until it had outlets in New York, Chicago, Baltimore, Detroit, and Louisville.

Railroad history in the United States up to the time of the Civil War separates naturally into four

A canalboat is hauled over the mountains, from one river to another, on a portage railway in the Alleghenies. As canals pushed west, many portage lines were built.

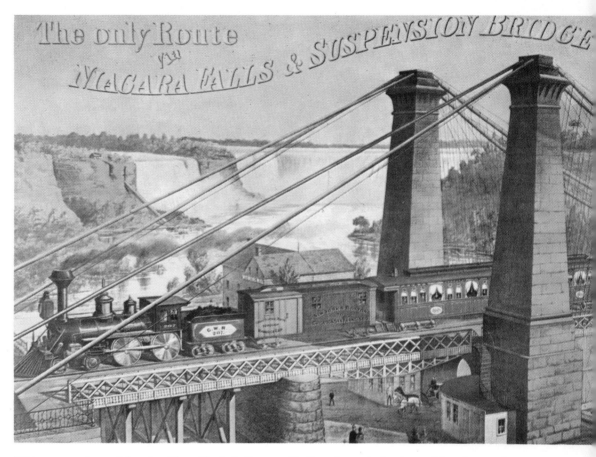

This poster issued by the New York & Boston Railroad reminds the public that only one route will take them west and at the same time give them a view of Niagara Falls.

ten-year periods. In the decade from 1820 to 1830 only forty miles of track were built.

By 1835, there were more than 200 railroad lines in the planning or construction stages, and 1,000 miles of track in actual operation. By 1850, there were 9,022 miles of operating railways, with the biggest increases in New York, Pennsylvania, and the New England States; and railroad investments reached $372,000,000.

In the next ten years, between 1850-60, the California Gold Rush and a new congressional policy of offering free land grants to railroad companies stimulated the westward movement of tracks. By 1860, about one billion dollars had been invested in American railroads, with $200,000,000 (or one-fifth of the total) coming from England and other European countries.

When the Civil War broke out, there were three times as many miles of track in operation as there had been ten years before—or a total of 31,246 miles of iron rails.

25

THE RAILROAD IN THE CIVIL WAR

General William Tecumseh Sherman once observed that "no army dependent on wagons can operate more than a hundred miles from its base, because the teams going and coming consume the contents of their wagons." If the horses would eat a whole wagonload of oats in a two hundred mile round trip, there would be no room left in the wagon for freight.

Then, just one hundred years ago, something new was added to the science of war. For the first time in history, whole armies, with all their equipment, could be transported hundreds of miles by rail.

By 1860, the United States had 30,000 miles of railway tracks, but only 10,000 miles of railroad were in the eleven Southern states. Few people on either side realized how great an advantage this gave the Union, whose 20,000 miles of track reached deep into the Middle West.

President Abraham Lincoln had been an attorney for the Illinois Central Railroad before he went into the White House. He knew how valuable the railroads would be in the struggle to defeat the Confederate States.

The President made Herman Haupt, formerly the general manager of the Pennsylvania Railroad, a colonel in the Union Army. Haupt was asked to run the railroads in occupied Virginia. Some of the Union generals did not like the idea of taking orders from a mere colonel. During the Second Battle of Bull Run one high-ranking officer halted several trains loaded with supplies for the front and told the engineers to be ready to carry him and his troops to another location. For twen-

The Union's Colonel Daniel C. McCallum ran the railroads in occupied Virginia.

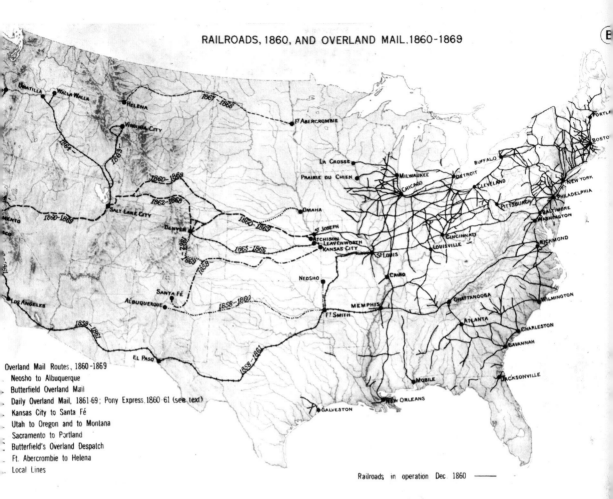

Overland Mail Routes, 1860-1869
Neosho to Albuquerque
Butterfield Overland Mail
Daily Overland Mail, 1861-69; Pony Express.1860-61 (see text)
Kansas City to Santa Fé
Utah to Oregon and to Montana
Sacramento to Portland
Butterfield's Overland Despatch
Ft. Abercrombie to Helena
Local Lines

Railroads in operation Dec. 1860 ————

This map shows how few railroad lines the South had in 1860 in comparison with those in the North. Notice that the West has stagecoach lines, but no railroads.

ty-four hours these locomotives stood on the main line, blocking all rail movements in either direction.

The story also is told of a military train halted at the order of a Union general, whose wife, traveling with him, grew weary and wished to stop for the night at a nearby farmhouse. The general saw nothing improper in this. What difference did it make if the journey of a few hundred ordinary soldiers was delayed a few hours? He did not realize that by stopping the train he shut off the only supply line for the whole Union army in Virginia.

After this, Haupt received a telegram from Secretary of War Stanton, asking that he "be as patient as possible with the Generals. Some of them probably will trouble you more than they will the enemy." The Secretary then threatened instant dismissal from the service for any Union officer interfering with the railroad operation.

The Union Army was the first to realize how the enemy could be

27

The Civil War saw America's first use of railroads for transporting troops to war. The upper section of this historical lithograph shows an embarkation cen-

ter in Philadelphia in 1861; a local regiment is getting ready to board a troop train. The pictures below show the washroom, free dining room, and kitchen.

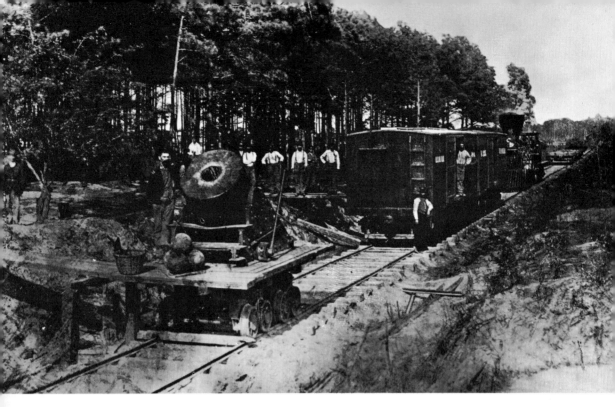

The Union's 17,000-pound mortar, The Dictator, *was so huge that it had to be mounted on a flatcar in order to move into battle position; it fired 200-pound shells.*

caught off guard by the sudden movement of troops by railroad. On June 2, 1861, in West Virginia, about 1,600 troops were put aboard a Baltimore & Ohio train at Grafton, and sent by rail to a point six miles east of town where they left the train and started marching south to Philippi. That night another 1,400 men left Grafton by train for Webster, several miles to the west. Once there, they also headed on foot for Philippi, planning to join forces with the first group and trap the Southern forces in a pincers at dawn the next morning. The Confederates were warned just in time to escape capture. But the Union forces took Philippi, and so won the first victory in United States military history in

which the railroads played a significant part.

In the South, General Robert E. Lee made use of the Confederate rail network to bring supplies and reinforcements to Virginia from as far as southeast Texas. In the summer of 1862, General Braxton Bragg took the Army of Tennessee from Tupelo, Mississippi, to Chattanooga, Tennessee, by rail. This allowed Bragg's Confederate soldiers to chase Union troops out of Tennessee and to enter Kentucky.

In September, 1863, the Confederate Army of Tennessee was battling much stronger Union forces in north Georgia, just below Chattanooga. Five brigades of infantry from Longstreet's First Corps in northern Virginia came to the rescue, traveling 900 miles by way of Wilmington, Augusta, and Atlanta. They arrived in time to swing victory to the South in the great Battle of Chickamauga.

This battle left Union troops at Chattanooga in a dangerous position. The nearest Northern force that could be spared for their relief was in Virginia. But the territory between was strongly held by Confederate forces.

Secretary Stanton called in Colonel Daniel C. McCallum, in prewar days the general superintendent of the New York & Erie Railroad. In one week, McCallum moved 23,000 men, with their horses, wagons, tents, cannons, and ammunition, over a roundabout route leading through Wheeling, Indianapolis, Louisville, Nashville, and last to a Union railhead at Bridgeport, Alabama. It was a remarkable feat, since the movement had to be made over tracks of at least three different gauges, or widths, where the wheels of one railroad's cars would not fit on the tracks of another. The troops crossed the Ohio River on a temporary floating bridge made of coal barges. They rescued the Union soldiers at Chattanooga, and McCallum was made a general.

During the first few months of the Civil War, armed clashes between the North and South did not occur very often. Life went on much as usual in 1861 in many border areas except when guerilla bands from one side or the other would stage raids.

This railway trestle across the Potomac replaced a bridge burned earlier in the war. President Lincoln said it looked as if it were made of "string and bean poles."

The raiders always tried to destroy all the railroad property they found. If they had time, they would tear up a section of track, build a roaring bonfire of ties, and pile the iron rails on top. Soon the rails would get red-hot, and sag down into grotesque shapes.

The Baltimore & Ohio Railroad suffered much damage from Confederate sympathizers. They swooped down on its tracks in Maryland from nearby Virginia so often, that at last the company built the first armored car ever seen on any railroad. With its cannon muzzle poking through a hole in front, this ironclad monster was used on many a raider caught in the act of burning a B & O trestle.

The great Civil war historian, Douglas Southall Freeman, said railroad routes in the battle areas "meant more than the mountain ranges and scarcely less than the great rivers in determining the lines of advance and defense." The iron horse was doing more to change warfare than anything since the invention of gunpowder.

One bold plan to destroy a vital railroad supply line serving the Confederate Army led to the famous Andrews Raid. On an April morning in 1862, the Western & Atlantic loco-

The General, *seized by Union agents, pulls out of Big Shanty, signaling the start of the great locomotive chase.*

motive, *General*, puffed into Marietta, Georgia, at the head of a passenger train bound from Atlanta to Chattanooga. When the train stopped, a party of men in civilian clothes climbed aboard. They told the conductor, Captain W. A. Fuller, that they were on their way to join the Confederate Army.

Eight miles west of Marietta, the train stopped again so passengers and crew could have breakfast at the Big Shanty Hotel. Captain Fuller looked up from his plate in surprise to see the *General* and three boxcars go flying off without him. Immediately he guessed that the stran-

gers were Union raiders, and with two other members of the train crew, he ran down the track in pursuit.

Once out of sight the commander of the Union party, a brave Kentuckian named James J. Andrews, stopped the *General* long enough to cut the telegraph wires, tear up a section of track behind him, and load the ties and rails into the last car.

Meanwhile, Captain Fuller and his men had found a small four-wheeled track car. Now one man could ride and rest while the other two ran and pushed.

In Etowah, they found an old engine, the *Yonah*, with steam up. Climbing aboard, they set out after the *General* at sixty miles an hour. But the ancient *Yonah* could not stand this dizzy pace for long, and Captain Fuller abandoned it, and continued the chase first in the *Shorter*, and then, at Adairsville in a newer engine, the *Texas*. The chase continued more cautiously now because the Yankees in the *General* were dropping ties on the tracks, in hope of derailing Fuller in the *Texas*.

Two miles past Calhoun, Fuller spotted the smoke of the *General*. Between Ringgold and Graysville the *General* ran out of cordwood and steam pressure dropped. Andrews and his men jumped off, after having been chased nearly ninety-one

Union troops burn an important railroad bridge across the Rappahannock in 1863.

miles, and left the *General* to roll along empty.

Fuller saw the Yankees scurrying for the woods. He kept going, until he reached the *General* and shoved it into Ringgold. There he found a company of mounted militia, and went hunting for the fugitives. All twenty-two were captured. Andrews and seven others were executed as spies; six were sent back to Union lines in an exchange of prisoners; and eight more went to prison in Atlanta from which they later escaped.

The Andrews Raid had failed. But Congress was so impressed by the bravery of the raiders that it voted each of them the Congressional Medal of Honor.

However, the story of the *General* was not yet finished. On June 27, 1864, it hauled a trainload of ammunition to Confederate troops fighting at Kennesaw Mountain, and that

night brought the wounded to Marietta. When the Confederates at last were forced to pull out of Atlanta, the *General* carried the last trainload of refugees.

The real victims of guerrilla raids on railroads were the weary repair crews who had to rebuild tracks and bridges after each "visit." At first, the raiders simply ripped up the rails and threw them in the ditch. This made it quite easy for repair workers to put them back in place. Rails that had been given the bonfire treatment were no great problem, either. Blacksmiths would build up the fires, reheat the rails, and hammer them back into shape.

The guerrillas learned to heat a rail to a glowing red, pick it up with tongs, and wrap it like a pretzel around the trunk of a stout tree. To salvage such a rail meant first cutting down the tree.

Bridges were also favorite targets for raiders, since repair crews had trouble finding iron beams or timbers of the proper size to restore ruined bridges.

No railroad was more badly damaged in the Civil War than the Louisville & Nashville. Most of the L & N's 269 miles of tracks were in Kentucky. And in 1861, Kentucky hoped to remain on friendly terms with both the North and the South. The rest of the L & N's rails were in Tennessee, which was sympathetic to the South, although it had not yet seceded from the Union.

This made the L & N a neutral railroad, with links to both sides. For a few months it did a rushing business, transferring food, clothing, and other military necessities from suppliers in the North to warehouses in the South.

Late in June, 1861, Tennessee withdrew from the Union and joined the other ten Confederate states. Tennessee's Governor Isham Harris confiscated all L & N track and rolling stock within its borders. Then Confederate troops led by General Buckner invaded southern Kentucky. He captured L & N trackage all the way to Lebanon Junction. The railroad was left with only thirty miles

At the top of the embankment at right stands Herman Haupt, a construction engineer who served the Union as chief repairman and builder of military railroads.

General Sherman (mounted) wrecked many miles of Georgia's railroads on his march to the sea. The track he is destroying here is the old-fashioned strap-rail type.

of main line and one-fourth of its cars and locomotives. When Union General William T. Sherman came storming down with the Kentucky Home Guards, Confederates retreated to the Green River, destroying tracks and bridges as they went.

In 1862, the Union Army began a drive toward Nashville. As the Southerners backed out of Kentucky into Tennessee, they took pains to demolish the L & N as they went. But railroad repair crews trudged along behind the troops, and by April had it in full operation all the way to Nashville.

Soon raids by Colonel John Hunt Morgan and his cavalry, and the campaigns of Bragg and Buell destroyed the L & N for a second time. So repairmen picked up their tools and began the weary job of rebuilding their railroad once again.

The new importance of railroads in military strategy was shown most clearly during General Sherman's advance into Georgia in 1864. His campaign was termed by railway historian Robert S. Henry as "the final, deciding act of the Confederate War."

Sherman's problem was to keep 100,000 troops and 35,000 animals supplied with ammunition and food during his 196-day drive through enemy territory to Atlanta. Everything the army needed had to come over a single-track railroad from Louisville, via Nashville and Chattanooga. Every day, General McCallum's train crews delivered 160 carloads of supplies and reinforcements to the front lines, taking the empty trains back promptly to be reloaded. After the fighting had ended, General Sherman wrote that his famous march through Georgia would have been "impossible without the railroads."

The railroads of both North and South paid a heavy price for assisting their armed forces. Some sections of trackage in the battle areas were destroyed and rebuilt as much as a dozen times. In all, General McCallum's men repaired 641 miles of track and 26 miles of bridges to keep the trains running.

There are some who say that the South, if it had seceded from the Union ten years earlier—before steel rails crossed the Appalachians —might still be known as the Confederate States of America. About that, no one can be certain; but we can be sure that superior Union rail strength helped defeat the Confederacy; and that the railroad made lasting changes in the science of modern warfare.

This photograph, taken in 1865 by Matthew Brady, the Civil War's master photographer, shows a ruined steam engine in the war-torn city of Richmond.

Thomas Hill painted this official picture of the driving of the Golden Spike.

THE GOLDEN SPIKE

In the middle of 1862, no one could be sure which side would win the Civil War. The Battle of Gettysburg was still a year away. Although their first concern was the terrible conflict dividing the North and the South, President Abraham Lincoln and Congress also took time to think about the future of the West. On July 1, 1862, President Lincoln signed the Pacific Railroad Act, that would begin the building of the first transcontinental railway from Omaha, Nebraska to Sacramento, California.

Two new companies were chartered for this big job. The Central Pacific was to start at Sacramento and come east over the Sierra Nevada Mountains. The Union Pacific

The ceremony took place near the tent city of Promontory, Utah, on May 10, 1869.

was to head west up the valley of the Platte River toward the Rockies. Somewhere in the desert plateau between these great barriers the two rail lines would meet.

Many months were needed to assemble materials and workmen, and it was January 8, 1863, before the Central Pacific laid its first rail. Three weeks later its first locomotive, the diamond-stacked *Governor Stanford*, chugged proudly up and down a few hundred yards of track.

The new railroad published its first timetable on June 6, 1864, announcing freight and passenger service over thirty-one miles of trackage from Sacramento to Newcastle.

Closer and closer moved the two railheads, and at last, on May 10, 1869, after more than five years of hardships and adventure, the tracks met in the Utah desert north of Great Salt Lake. After the last spike had been hammered into place, a Central Pacific wood-burning loco-

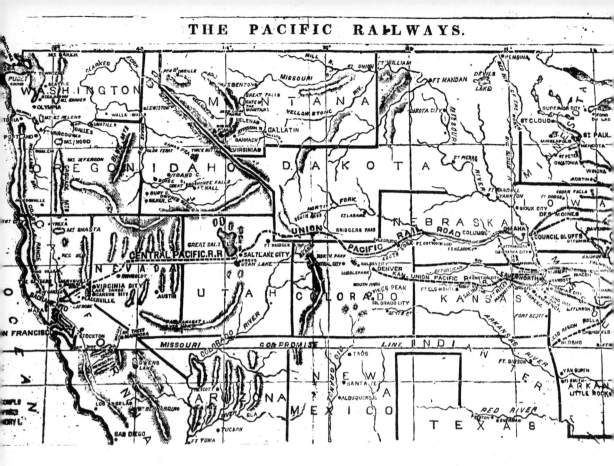

On January 18, 1867, the New York Tribune *printed this map of the proposed route.*

motive, the *Jupiter*, puffed up to touch the Union Pacific's coal-burning *No. 119.* A Sacramento photographer, Colonel Charles Savage, recorded the historic moment on a glass negative with his camera. When Bret Harte, the western author, saw the photograph he wrote the famous poem which begins:

> *What was it the Engines said,*
> *Pilots touching, head to head,*
> *Facing on a single track,*
> *Half a world behind each back?*

If locomotives could talk, they might very well have spoken of great difficulties overcome by the two construction gangs as the tracks were pushed through the wilderness. Except for wooden ties which could be cut out of the Sierra forests, all the Central Pacific's rails, locomotives, cars, and other supplies had to make the 15,000 mile voyage by sea, around Cape Horn, from the East. To build a railroad grade through the Sierras—a range of jagged peaks and deep canyons, lashed by storms —the CP's tracklayers had only picks and shovels, mule-drawn carts and scrapers, and black powder.

As for the Union Pacific, when it began work, no eastern railroad had yet come within two hundred miles of Omaha. The first UP rails and rolling stock arrived in Omaha aboard freight wagons. Its ties had to be cut in forests far to the north and floated down the Missouri River, for the Platte Valley had no suitable timber. Hostile Indians often attacked construction camps, killing workers and destroying supplies. There were no good surveys of the routes the two railroad companies were to follow. Engineering teams risked being scalped by Indians as they searched for passes through the mountains.

A little weekly newspaper in Michigan—the Ann Arbor *Emigrant*—was probably the first to suggest a transcontinental railway in 1832.

In Boston, Dr. Samuel Barlow, a surgeon, wrote a series of pamphlets urging construction of an overland railroad from Cape Cod to the mouth of the Columbia River.

Asa Whitney, a retired shipowner who had made a fortune in the China trade, spent all his money touring the country, trying to win public support for a bill in Congress to construct a railroad. The line was to run west from Wisconsin across the Plains to the Rockies, down the Lewis and Clark trail along the Clearwater and Columbia rivers, and to end at Puget Sound.

Congress studied this bill in 1845, 1846, and 1847. But it was blocked by the powerful Senator Thomas H. Benton of Missouri, who insisted that the railroad must start from St. Louis, Missouri.

Railroad surveyors scale a cliff in the Uinta mountains of Utah as they map terrain for CP roadbed construction.

41

Cheyenne Indians, seeking to stop the advance of railroads through their ancestral hunting grounds in Kansas in 1867, tear up the rails and burn the ties. The

But Senator Benton's plan had no better success. For now Congress began to argue over where its terminals should be located. Southern congressmen thought the railroad should start in some Southern seaport such as Baltimore, Charleston, or Savannah. They blocked efforts to name a Northern city as the terminus. But the railroad could not be built without Northern money, and this could be had only for the construction of a northern route.

When the Civil War began, Southern members of Congress went home. In their absence, it was easy

railroad brought with it not only settlers but also white hunters who disturbed the migrating herds of buffalo and slaughtered the beasts in great numbers.

for Northern members to agree that a transcontinental railroad over a northern route was needed. It would help keep California and Oregon loyal to the Union, they argued. And the name given to one of the companies chartered in the Pacific Railroad Act—the Union Pacific—shows the state of Congress' sympathies in the year 1862.

President Lincoln chose Omaha as the eastern terminus of the railroad. His choice was probably the result of a talk he had had four years before with General Grenville M. Dodge, chief engineer of the Union

A Union Pacific construction train of 1868 carried men, track, and supplies.

Pacific. General Dodge met Mr. Lincoln by chance at Council Bluffs, Iowa, in 1859. The man who was to be the next President of the United States had listened carefully as General Dodge told him that the best route across the Great Plains was up the 600-mile-long valley of the Platte River. This route led to a natural pass through the Rockies, at their lowest elevation.

Later, when construction actually began, General Dodge had a hard time organizing his track-laying gangs. So many able-bodied men of the North were serving in the Union Army that he had to fill out the UP construction crews by importing immigrants from Ireland. The General had been warned that the flow of money from investors might be shut off unless he showed speedy progress. So he pushed his "Irish Terriers" hard. Here is how a correspondent for the *Fortnightly Review* described the scene at the end of track on the UP line:

"Tracklaying on the Union Pacific is a science, and we . . . hacked westward before that hurrying corps of sturdy operators with a mingled feeling of amusement, curiosity, and profound respect. On they came. A light car, drawn by a single horse, gallops up to the front with its load of rails. Two men seize the end of a rail and start forward, the rest of the gang taking hold by twos until it is clear of the car. They come forward at a run. At the word of command, the rail is dropped in its place, right side up, with care, while the same process goes on at the other side. . . . Less than 30 seconds to a rail for each gang, and four rails go down to the minute. Quick work, you say, but the fellows on the Union Pacific are tremendously in earnest.

"The moment the car is emptied, it is tipped over on its side of the track to let the next loaded car pass it, and then it is tipped back again; and it is a sight to see it go flying back for another load, propelled by a horse at full gallop at the end of sixty or eighty feet of rope, ridden by a young Jehu, who drives furiously.

"Close behind the first gang come the gaugers, spikers, and bolters, and a lively time they make of it. It is a grand Anvil Chorus that these sturdy sledges are playing across the Plains; it is in triple time, three strokes to a spike. There are ten spikes to a rail, four hundred rails to a mile, eighteen hundred miles to San Francisco—twenty-one million times are they to come down with their sharp punctuation before the great work of modern America is complete."

The correspondent had made his visit on one of the railroad's more peaceful days. For there were other days when General Dodge's men

The workers shown here were part of a Central Pacific construction gang; they were followed by gandy dancers or tarriers who spiked the rails to the ties.

had to take refuge in their supply trains and fight off Indian attacks.

In 1866, when the rails had been pushed some two hundred miles west of the Missouri River, Chief Spotted Tail and his Sioux braves decided the white man and his iron horse had gone far enough. They came war whooping down on Plum Creek, surrounded a handcar running ahead

fireman in the burning wreckage, they galloped off with plunder from the boxcars.

Surveying crews working ahead of the tracklayers usually were accompanied by a military escort of from ten to one hundred soldiers. In spite of the troops, the parties were often attacked.

The UP construction chief had his troubles. Whiskey peddlers, dance hall girls, and gamblers followed the supply trains. They built temporary tent cities on the prairie. Shootings and robbings became so common that the railroad had to take the law into its own hands.

One day word came to General Dodge that gamblers had invaded a construction camp and were "running wild." He telegraphed orders to his second in command, Jack Casement, to "clean house."

A few days later General Dodge arrived at the construction camp and asked for a report.

"There it is," said Casement, pointing to a row of new graves on the prairie. "The bad men died with their boots on."

Out in California the Central Pacific was having problems of a different kind. Where the UP had to

of a freight train as a pilot, and scalped the crewmen. Then they ripped up the track and derailed the following train. Leaving the tomahawked corpses of the engineer and

47

battle Indians and outlaws, the CP's progress was being slowed by rugged mountains and terrible storms. Try as they might, Central Pacific surveyors could not find an easy route across the Sierra Nevada mountains. They realized they would have to begin bridging and tunneling on a scale never before attempted in construction history.

But Charles Crocker, the CP's construction boss, was not to be stopped. If there was no low pass through the Sierras, he would go right over the top. He hired an army of Chinese laborers, and soon they were carving a path through the mountains. Over the steep cliffs of the American River, the Chinese would lower one of their number in a wicker basket tied to a rope. There he would dangle while he drilled a hole in the solid rock deep enough for a charge of black powder. After lighting the fuse, he would signal frantically to be hauled up. Seconds later, the explosion would punch out a few feet of ledge for the CP's rails.

When blizzards buried the roadbed under drifts thirty and forty feet deep, "Crocker's pets" went underground to dig a series of fourteen tunnels through peaks that could not be bypassed. One, at the summit of the Sierras, goes through 1,659 feet of solid rock.

Central Pacific workers set up camp in the vast spaces of Utah in 1869.

Despite these efforts, the Central Pacific's mileage of completed track seemed small. The Union Pacific was speedily working up the flat valley of the Platte. So, in the winter of 1866-67, Crocker had his pigtailed Chinese workers drag three locomotives, forty cars, and enough rail and spikes for forty miles of track across the top of the Sierras. There the equipment was hauled into the Truckee River canyon, where the snow cover was thinner and trackwork possible even in stormy weather. On November 13, 1867, CP locomotives reached the California-Nevada boundary, although seven miles of difficult construction remained behind them in the mountains.

Even after the job was finished, heavy snows blocked the tracks for many weeks each winter, cutting off the movement of supplies from Sacramento to the end of track. The CP's light engines and crude snowplows could not cut a path through such drifts.

Crocker hired battalions of loggers and carpenters, built sawmills high in the mountains, and began constructing snowsheds to protect his track. At last there were forty miles of these sheds along the route.

There was good reason for the Central Pacific's haste to reach the Nevada line. The 1862 Act named this point as the junction for the two rail lines. It also stated that the company arriving there first could keep on building track until it finally met the other. Since the federal government was sometimes paying up to $96,000 a mile, as well as giving them a 400-foot right of way through public lands, both companies were eager to build as much track as they could.

By the end of 1867, the Central Pacific and the Union Pacific no longer thought of themselves as partners. They were bitter rivals in a race for big stakes.

Now it was the UP's turn to deal with difficulties of mountain railroading. By November, 1867, its tracks were in Cheyenne. Just beyond lay the Black Hills, which rise steeply out of the plains surrounding Cheyenne, and drop just as abruptly to the flatlands of Laramie on the other side. For two years UP surveyors had failed to locate an easy route past this granite barrier. Finally General Dodge himself found one. Strangely enough, his Indian enemies helped him do it.

The UP boss was returning from a survey of the Powder River country when his small party of horsemen met a band of redskins at Lodge Pole Creek. The railroadmen hastily dismounted and took cover. Their rifles held off the Indians until nightfall. Then, through the darkness they led their horses quietly back along the way they had come. Dawn found them retreating down an unknown ridge which led to the Cheyenne plains. The delighted

America's first transcontinental train travels west on Union Pacific rails. This Currier and Ives print of 1869 pictures it stopping at a typical town on the prairie.

general told his companions they not only had saved their scalps, but also found the path for the Union Pacific over the Black Hills.

Once at Laramie, the Union Pacific had a new source of supply for wooden ties. Now timber could be floated down the streams from Rocky Mountain forests instead of being hauled eight hundred miles from the Missouri River. But forty carloads of rails, spikes, food, and ammunition still were needed every day to supply the crews at the end of the track. In 1868, General Dodge's 20,000 workers pushed the Union Pacific tracks across the Rockies, past Ogden, Utah, and on to remote Humboldt Wells.

Bitter winter caught the UP construction gangs in the Wasatch Mountains, but they would not be stopped. Tracks were laid on a roadbed of packed snow and ice. They would be relaid after the spring thaw, and in the meantime the line could go forward. But one mild day the ice melted just enough to be slippery, and an entire construction train is said to have slid—rails, ties, and all—into the ditch.

With the Wasatches at last behind them, UP crews, in the spring of 1869, lined their tracks straight out across the Utah desert, and then began sprinting for the finish line. The Central Pacific in 1869 had crossed the Nevada desert and had reached Utah's western border.

Word came to Crocker in early April that the Union Pacific had broken its previous record by laying eight miles of track in a single day.

Crocker snorted. "We can beat that," he said. "I'll bet ten thousand dollars my Chinese can lay ten miles of rail between daylight and dark."

Vice-President Thomas C. Durant of the Union Pacific promptly covered the bet, and Crocker began making careful plans. Ties were arranged on the graded right of way several miles ahead. Rails and spikes were stockpiled at intervals along the way. As dawn broke on April 28, 1869, Crocker's crews went into action, with the UP's General Dodge on hand to make sure there was no cheating. With the grace and precision of ballet dancers, the Chinese swung rails into place and pounded down the spikes. In a little less than twelve hours, the Central Pacific was ten miles and fifty-six feet longer than it had been the night before. Crocker won his bet, and his tracklaying record still stands.

Now locomotive whistles from both railroads could be heard on the shores of the Great Salt Lake. Rival surveying parties had long since passed each other in opposite directions, and soon grading crews were working alongside each other on

This travel poster announced the beginning of transcontinental railroad service.

Tents and shacks lined the Main Street at Promontory, Utah.

parallel roadbeds, sometimes only a few yards apart. The Union Pacific's Irishmen did not like the look of the Central Pacific's "heathen," and there were battles with fists and shovels.

Finally Congress realized that if it did not call a halt, the rival railroads might never stop laying track alongside each other. So the congressmen voted to fix Promontory Point, on the plateau north of the Great Salt Lake, as the official meeting place.

On the morning of May 10, Leland Stanford, governor of Cali-

fornia and president of the Central Pacific, chugged up to the ceremonial spot in a private train. The Union Pacific sent a train, too, with a large delegation. Not far from the tracks, the saloons in the brand new tent city of Promontory were doing a rushing business.

A happy, noisy crowd watched a squad of Chinese carry up a length of rail to close the last gap in the transcontinental railroad. An onlooker fired his pistol into the air, and the Chinese, thinking the Irish were after them again, dropped the rail and ran.

The historic Golden Spike is engraved with the names of key railroad officials.

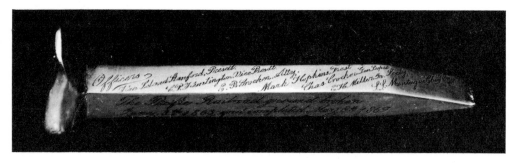

At last the rail was down on a polished laurel tie. It had been placed by the two construction superintendents, the UP's Samuel B. Reed and the CP's J. H. Strobridge. Governor Stanford stepped up with a silver sledge hammer and a solid gold spike. It was planned that Stanford and vice-president Durant of the Union Pacific would drive it home. The blows were to be signaled to every major city in the nation via coast-to-coast telegraphic hookup.

Unfortunately, neither Governor Stanford nor vice-president Durant seemed able to hit the Golden Spike with their silver sledges. Finally Jack Casement took over, and drove the spike home with the skill of long practice.

Then the telegraph hookup failed, and the historic clicks could not be heard past Omaha. A quick-thinking Western Union operator there saved the day by tapping out a duplicate set of clicks. These sounded real enough in New York, Boston, Philadelphia, and Washington, where they touched off the ringing of bells and a series of cannon salutes. The Pacific Railroad was completed at last.

When Governor Stanford saw a print of Colonel Savage's photograph, he was most unhappy. The

Compare this photograph of the actual ceremony at Promontory with the glamorous official painting shown at the beginning of the chapter.

A proud nation saw the American West linked to the rest of the country when the first transcontinental trains came down the mountains into San Francisco.

distinguished personages present at the Golden Spike ceremony, including himself, did not show up at all, while the "raffish, uncouth" people from the tent city of Promontory were far too visible for his liking.

Back in Sacramento, Governor Stanford commissioned a celebrated artist, Thomas Hill, to paint an idealized version of the events at Promontory Point. The drunks, gamblers, and dance hall girls of Promontory are nowhere to be seen. Ordinary railroad workers stand at a respectful distance while Governor Stanford poses with dignity between the rails in the company of Reverend John Todd. As for the Golden Spike, it was quickly removed from Promontory Point before some rascal from the tent city could steal it.

In 1904, a twelve mile trestle across the Great Salt Lake was finished, shortening the distance between Lucin and Ogden from 147 to 103 miles. Afterwards, only a few freights used the Promontory route. Then in World War II when steel rail was scarce, 120 miles of track between Lucin and Corinne were torn up to be relaid elsewhere.

Now, Promontory Point is almost as lonely as it was a century ago. Only a sagging frame building and a concrete monument remain to mark the spot where, on that spring day in 1869, two bands of iron came together in the Utah desert to join two halves of a nation.

Jim Fisk

Daniel Drew

Jay Gould

FABULOUS FINANCIERS

The heroes of early day American railroading were such practical mechanics as Peter Cooper, Horatio Allen, and Matthias Baldwin; men who knew how to build steam engines and make them chug along primitive rails made of wood and strap iron.

After these pioneers had shown how the newfangled steam cars could move passengers and freight faster and cheaper than stage coaches or canal barges, a new type of railroadman was needed. These were not inventors or engineers. They were businessmen who could take clusters of small, independent railways and unite them in big, smooth-running systems. One of the first of these new financiers was Erastus Corning, a manufacturer of

nails and a politician in Albany, New York. He thought it ridiculous that there should be ten individual railway companies between Albany and Buffalo, each operating a few dozen miles of track. In August, 1853, he formed the New York Central, assembling all these lines under one management.

Passenger and freight business increased greatly, and the Central promptly began yielding profits far greater than the previous total earnings of the ten small companies.

Cornelius Vanderbilt, some years later, was to take over this combined system and build it into a railroad covering almost the whole northeast section of the United States.

While still in his teens, Vanderbilt had started his career in the

Cornelius Vanderbilt

transportation business with the purchase of a Staten Island ferryboat. With the profits he earned, he bought more ferries, and soon was known around New York harbor as "the Commodore." Next he acquired some elegant side-wheel passenger steamers plying the Hudson River and Long Island Sound. He had piled up a fortune of ten million dollars by the time he decided to become a railroader.

Commodore Vanderbilt wanted to put together a combination of railroads running from New York City to the Great Lakes. He began his campaign in 1862, or earlier, by buying stock in two little railroads —the New York & Harlem, and the New York & Hudson. Once they

were in his control, the Commodore also controlled all rail traffic in and out of New York City.

Daniel Drew, boss of the rival Erie Railroad, was a rascally ex-cattle drover. He guessed what the Commodore was planning, but "Uncle Dan'l" hoped to discourage Vanderbilt by forcing up the price of New York & Harlem stock. As fast as Vanderbilt bought shares, Drew would offer more, many of which he did not really own. Speculators began grabbing Harlem stock, and soon the price soared from $15 to $179 a share. Then Vanderbilt demanded that Drew produce the stock certificates "Uncle Dan'l" had sold him. Drew was obliged to go out

This cartoon, Justice on the Rail, *shows the fall, in 1872, of Jay Gould (bottom) and his cohorts from control of the Erie.*

and buy them, at an inflated price, and deliver them to Vanderbilt. The Commodore had won his first round with the "tobacco-chewing, evil-faced country skinflint," Drew.

Vanderbilt next got control of the New York and Hudson line running north to Albany, where it joined the independently-owned New York Central. But the Central had an un-

derstanding with Hudson River steamboat lines, and would transfer its freight and passengers to Vanderbilt's New York & Harlem only in winter when the river was frozen and the river boats could not run.

The Commodore waited until winter before making the next move. Then, in mid-January, 1867, he gave orders to his trains to stop two miles

The first four steam engines used on Vanderbilt's New York Central Railroad appear in this poster issued in 1874.

agement. They were "Jubilee Jim" Fisk, an ex-peddler of kitchenware and notions in Vermont, and Jay Gould, a shrewd speculator in railroad stocks. They let word get to Vanderbilt that he might be able to buy enough Erie stock to get control, and thus be rid of that rival railroad.

The Commodore took the bait, but as soon as he began buying Erie stock, Fisk, Gould, and Drew began issuing new shares. Vanderbilt continued to buy, and the price of Erie stock soared to dizzy heights on the Stock Exchange.

Now Vanderbilt went to court to force Drew to quit printing false stock. But Drew and his pals escaped the court order by fleeing to Brooklyn with the Erie's money, where they kept on printing bogus stock.

The public became so angry with Drew, Fisk, and Gould that not even the corrupt politicians they had bribed could protect them any longer. They loaded the Erie's cash and records aboard a chartered ferryboat and slipped across the Hudson to safety in New Jersey.

Vanderbilt next had a New York judge declare the Erie bankrupt.

Drew decided to sue for peace. He said he would resign as Erie's treasurer, permit the Erie and the Central to merge, and repay Vanderbilt for the false stock. The Commodore thought he had won at last.

short of the Albany depot on the east side of the river. Passengers had to walk through the snow to change trains. As a result, the New York Central's profits and stock value dropped sharply, and Vanderbilt promptly bought the Central.

Drew vowed to get even with Vanderbilt. To do this, he brought two sharp-witted friends into Erie man-

This cartoon made fun of the race for power between Vanderbilt (left) and Fisk.

But the wily "Uncle Dan'l" had still more tricks up his sleeve. He sent Jay Gould to the New York legislature with a bill to legalize all the fake Erie stock, and to forbid the merger of the two railroads. Gould gave $180,000 worth of stock to some dishonest legislators in Albany, and the bill became law.

Drew's triumph was brief, for he quarreled with his partners, and threw his entire fortune into a fight with Fisk and Gould for control of the Erie. He lost. Daniel Drew, who once had thrown down three million dollars in cash to take over the Erie railroad, died a beggar.

Commodore Vanderbilt never lost the New York Central. At his death in 1877, control passed to his son, William Henry Vanderbilt, and the Commodore's fortune was estimated at seventy-five million dollars.

In the West, also, the big job of pushing rails across the Plains to the Pacific attracted a number of dishonest, as well as honest builders. This time federal money was involved, rather than private fortunes; and this time the bribery and corruption stretched all the way to the national Capitol.

One of the most scandalous chapters in American history involves the part played by the Crédit Mobilier, a construction company hired to build 667 miles of track in Utah, for the Union Pacific Railroad.

In 1864, Thomas C. Durant, Oakes Ames, and other important Union Pacific stockholders purchased the charter of the Crédit Mobilier. The

Union Pacific had been granted enough land by the federal government to more than cover the cost of laying the tracks. But Crédit Mobilier overcharged the UP so outrageously, for construction, that the railroad went into debt. Stockholders of Crédit Mobilier made profits totaling over twenty million dollars.

Later, valuable Crédit Mobilier shares were given to a number of congressmen, in hope that the track-laying scandal would never come to light. But all the names of the congressmen who accepted shares were published in 1872, in the New York *Sun*.

When Congress investigated, those involved were censured, and the UP continued laying tracks westward.

These financial shenanigans made people suspicious of railroads and those who ran them. But the fat profits earned by the "steamcars" encouraged many new companies to lay rails into the virgin territory yet remaining.

Rails were going down far too swiftly. Tracks were poking out into wilderness areas where homesteaders would not settle for years to come. These railroads needed profits to pay their debts, but there would be none until the Indians

could be removed, and their lands settled by farmers and ranchers.

These were the circumstances which helped bring on the great financial panic of 1873, in which scores of railways suffered bankruptcy. One of these new roads—with too many Indians and not enough money—was the Northern Pacific Railway, chartered by Congress in 1864 to build a line from Lake Superior to Puget Sound.

To help it sell stock, the federal government gave the NP 25,600 acres of public land for each mile of track laid in U. S. territories along its route. Today such vast lands would have enormous value, but in those days the NP's territory was inhabited only by Indians and a few trappers. By 1873 it owned 500 unprofitable miles of track. In the Panic of 1873, it failed.

A year later an effort was made

A cartoonist hits at the greed of railroad tycoons in this drawing labeled Let Them Have It All And Be Done With It. *Vanderbilt, Gould, and others cut up Manhattan; another tries to buy Europe.*

The Erie Railroad, advertised in this poster, was the prize in the desperate Vanderbilt-Fisk struggle for control.

to resume construction. But across the Minnesota line, in Dakota territory, lived the hostile Sioux Indians. They had seen how the Union Pacific had pushed their Cheyenne brothers off the Plains to the south. Should they let the NP drive iron rails into the heart of Sioux country? Never, said Chiefs Red Cloud and Sitting Bull.

Once across the Minnesota border, the NP's Swedish and Norwegian tracklayers ran into a hail of arrows. They put down their shovels and sledges and quit. They had signed on to build a railroad, not to fight Indians. Until the United States Cavalry cleared the way, the Northern Pacific could not move.

Down in St. Louis, General W. T. Sherman, Army Commander for the West, was sympathetic. "I think our interest is to favor the undertaking of the Road," he said, "as it will help to bring the Indian problem to a final solution."

President Ulysses S. Grant told Sherman not to attack. Instead, the Great White Father would send a peace commission to treat with the Sioux and settle matters without bloodshed.

Sherman knew better, but he was a good soldier and followed orders. The peace commission came and

went, and the Indian ravagings continued. Then came the bloody incident that sent the U. S. Army into action against the Sioux.

On June 25, 1876, Lieutenant Colonel George A. Custer, leading a

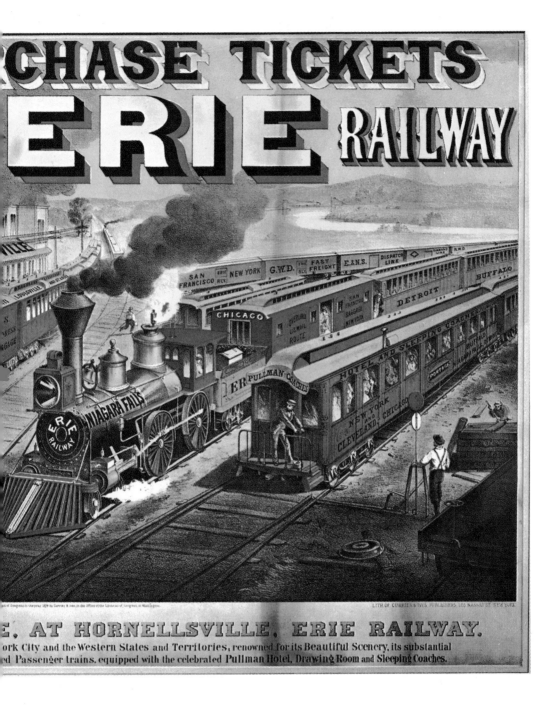

troop of the Seventh Cavalry along the Little Big Horn River in Montana Territory, ran headlong into a large band of Sioux and Cheyenne. By nightfall, Custer and all of his soldiers had been killed.

Now the public howled for revenge. Colonel Ranald S. Mackenzie, leader of Mackenzie's Raiders on the Rio Grande border, hurried north with the Fourth Cavalry. In September, he surrounded a Sioux

63

Leland Stanford

Collis Huntington

Horse and all his followers gave themselves up. The Sioux war was over and the Northern Pacific had a clear road to the Pacific. In September, 1883, the rails reached Tacoma, in Washington Territory.

In the meantime, a Scottish steamboatman from Canada, James Jerome Hill, had become a railroading man. He set out to build a line north of the Northern Pacific, from St. Paul to Seattle. Sheer lunacy, said the experts. If the NP already was in trouble because its tracks were too far north of the wheat-

camp and captured Chief Red Cloud. In October, he swooped down on a village of the Northern Cheyennes on the Powder River, killing forty braves and capturing six hundred horses. In the tepees, Mackenzie found relics of the Custer massacre: scalps, regimental flags, and letters taken from the bodies of cavalrymen. Custer was avenged.

That winter the Indians learned that Generals Nelson Miles and George Crook were planning a two-pronged attack to catch the remaining northern Indians in a vise. The armies would move after the spring thaw. Straggling bands of Indians began to turn up at army posts to surrender. On May 6, 1877, Crazy

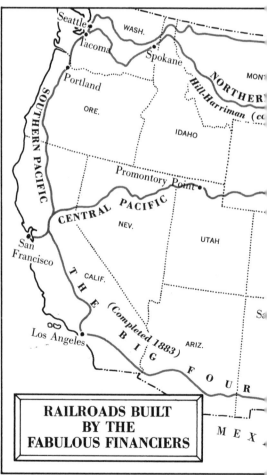

RAILROADS BUILT BY THE FABULOUS FINANCIERS

growing country, where would Hill's Great Northern get its revenues? And besides, how could anyone build a transcontinental railroad without free public lands or federal aid?

But Jim Hill did it. By 1893— ten years after the NP crossed the Cascade Range—Great Northern tracks were in Seattle, and its trains were earning money. "Hill's Folly" had become Hill's triumph. Hill sent agents to the East Coast to develop a market for Douglas fir lumber, which he could haul from

Charles Crocker

Mark Hopkins

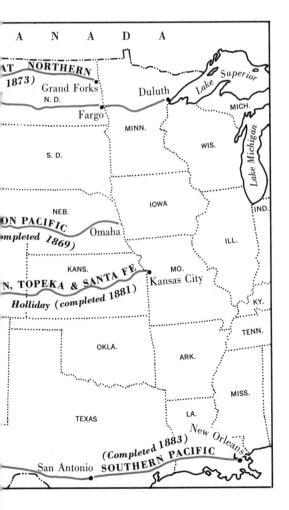

the West Coast. He bought a fleet of ocean-going steamers and sent salesmen to the Orient to find out which of the products of New England factories could be laid down at a profit on the docks of Yokohama and Shanghai, via the Great Northern.

Cyrus Holliday, another determined railroad builder, pushed the Santa Fe across the prairie during the worst of the Panic of 1873.

Young Holliday had come out of Pennsylvania to find a good place to grow potatoes, and established the city of Topeka, Kansas, in 1854.

This map shows the rail empires of the West's financiers—Stanford, Hill, Crocker, Huntington, Hopkins, and Harriman.

By February 9, 1880, the Atchison, Topeka & Santa Fe railway reached Santa Fe, New Mexico, and Cyrus Holliday's dream of delivering Kansas potatoes to the great Southwest had come true.

The years just after the Civil War were difficult for the railways of the South. The big Pennsylvania railroad took over some of the southern railways nearest its territory and improved them. But the Pennsylvania soon lost interest, and for another ten years southern railway development proceeded very slowly.

Next, a southern financier, Calvin S. Brice, put together a group of railways extending from the Atlantic coast cities to Cincinnati, Ohio, and Shreveport, Louisiana. The Brice system survived for a few years, but went bankrupt during the 1893 financial panic.

Real recovery for the railways of the former Confederacy dates from about 1895, when the Wall Street banker, J. P. Morgan, stepped in and organized the Southern Railroad System. Millions were spent on tracks, trestles, bridges, repair shops, and rolling stock.

Around the turn of the century two other large rail systems—the Atlantic Coast Line and the Seaboard Air Line—came into existence. These railroads were most important in reviving the agriculture, industry, and prosperity of the war-torn South.

THE SCOURGE OF THE WEST.
"Hold up your hands."

Far out in California, the postwar railroad-building boom aroused ambitions in the four men who were to organize the Central Pacific. Leland Stanford, Mark Hopkins, Charles Crocker, and Collis P. Huntington were moderately successful Sacramento shopkeepers when the chance came along to help build the first transcontinental railroad. When pro-

67

Edward H. Harriman

Henry Villard

Jim Hill

fits from their half of the Pacific railroad began pouring into Sacramento banks, the quartet lost interest in shopkeeping. They became the famous "Big Four" of western railroading. Why should they wait for eastern investors to come in and develop more railroads in their own home state? They would go ahead and build them themselves.

Soon the construction crews of the newly-organized Southern Pacific railway were moving into the empty San Joaquin Valley, founding such cities as Fresno, Merced, Modesto, and Tulare as they moved southward from Oakland.

The Southern Pacific's owners pondered whether it would be worthwhile to go out of their way to stop at the sleepy little city of Los Angeles. Ten thousand people lived there, and it did not seem likely that it would attract many more settlers. When the citizens persuaded the railroad that southern California might amount to something someday, the SP swung west, in 1872, to put Los Angeles on the main line.

Now the Southern Pacific turned to the east and by December, 1880, the rails were in Deming, New Mexico, meeting the Santa Fe and giving the United States its second transcontinental route.

The ambitions of the "Big Four" soared higher. Why not keep on driving east, to the Gulf of Mexico? On went the Southern Pacific tracklayers. By 1883, after a series of mergers, SP trains were running all the way from San Francisco to New Orleans; and by 1885 a fleet of steamers flying the SP flag were carrying passengers and freight the rest of the way to New York.

While all this was going on, the pioneer city of Portland, Oregon, began to feel that Progress had neglected her.

The Oregon & California railroad had been started in 1868 to link Portland and Marysville, California, but it was not getting along very fast.

Unhappy German and Dutch bondholders dispatched Henry Villard, a Bavarian journalist, to see what had happened to their investments in the O & C and the NP. He formed the Oregon Railroad & Navigation Company, intending to bring the Northern Pacific into Portland. But Villard had the bad habit of trying to please his investors with big dividends before his railroads were earning enough to pay them. In 1883, he lost the two halves of the Oregon & California to the Southern Pacific, which promptly joined them. And in 1893, he was ousted from the Northern Pacific, and Jim Hill and J. P. Morgan took over.

Next it was the turn of the mighty Union Pacific to have more financial difficulties. Its builders lost interest in their railroad after the Golden Spike ceremony at Promontory cut off the flow of federal construction money. Those twenty millions which had been pocketed by the Crédit Mobilier conspirators were loans that Uncle Sam expected the railroad to pay back from earnings. So, when the financial panic of 1893 caught the Union Pacific with a debt burden of $53,000,000, the company collapsed.

A second-generation financier, Edward H. Harriman, boss of the prosperous Illinois Central, bought the run-down Union Pacific and rebuilt it from end to end, laying heavier rail, easing curves and grades, and buying dozens of powerful new locomotives. With the Illinois Central giving it a terminal in Chicago, the Union Pacific was back in business, stronger than ever.

Now Harriman laid plans to gobble up the vast Southern Pacific. Huntington staved off the merger while he lived, but a year after his death in 1900, the SP became a Harriman property.

In the meantime, Harriman had picked up the Oregon Short Line and Henry Villard's old Oregon Railroad & Navigation line down the south bank of the Columbia into Portland. Then Harriman learned that Jim Hill also had plans for railroad development in Oregon.

Hill meant business. He sent skilled engineers, disguised as trout fishermen, to make surveys of the canyon of the Deschutes River, which flows into the Columbia River. Soon Hill had a small army blasting

out a right of way and laying track up the Deschutes.

Harriman was recovering from an appendicitis operation when he heard about Hill's invasion of Oregon. Instantly Harriman guessed what Hill was planning to do.

In a few days Harriman tracklayers were also heading up the Des-

chutes, on the opposite bank. Rival crews fought it out with fists and pick handles and occasional charges of dynamite. And in Wall Street, Hill and Harriman battled for control of the Northern Pacific, sending its stock soaring to a thousand dollars a share.

On the construction front, Harri-

joint management of the Northern Pacific, and agreed to joint use of the Deschutes River trackage. Thus ended America's most famous big railroad battle.

Harriman, however, was not the man to relax. He was determined to accomplish what no other railroader, before or since, had been able to do: to run trains under one management from the Atlantic to the Pacific.

By 1907, he controlled the Illinois Central, UP, and SP, and began buying large amounts of B & O and New York Central stock. The United States government feared that if Harriman succeeded in his coast-to-coast plans, he might set up a nation-wide rail monopoly.

Then, in 1909, Harriman's sudden death put an end to his dream. With him died the greatest of all United States railroad empires. The American public did not want any single company to have so much power over the movement of passengers and freight. The federal government went to court and broke apart the Union Pacific and the Southern Pacific. Next, the Union Pacific board of directors voluntarily relinquished control of the B & O, breaking up the coast-to-coast combination—and the era of fabulous financiers was at an end.

man tricked Hill by purchasing a piece of property which controlled the only outlet from the canyon to the plateau. But Hill thwarted Harriman's effort to buy a controlling interest in Northern Pacific.

At last, the two tycoons were obliged to bury the hatchet. They formed a new company to exercise

THE WILD WEST

When the first railroad crossed the Mississippi River, the Great Plains were covered from Texas to Canada with vast herds of bison, or American buffalo.

In the late sixties and early seventies it seemed that everyone who followed the Union Pacific, the Kansas Pacific, and the Santa Fe railroads into the prairie country wanted the buffalo killed off. Soldiers said they could not tame the hostile Plains Indians as long as the red men could depend on the buffalo herds for food. Cattlemen wanted to run longhorns on the big natural pasture occupied by the buffalo.

Professional buffalo hunters were at work on the Plains in the years just after the Civil War, providing meat for railroad construction camps and selling a few buffalo robes. But the slaughter of the buffalo did not begin in earnest until 1871, when word came of a market for buffalo hides in England.

Until this time, white men had considered buffalo skins to be almost worthless. The hide was too spongy to make good shoes or saddles. Then English tanners found they could make fine, soft leather coats from it. These became popular with European army officers, who called them "buffe" coats, and the tanneries said they would buy all the buffalo hides America could produce.

The big buffalo hunt was on. Carrying heavy, muzzle-loading .50 calibre Sharps rifles, hunters would creep up within fifty yards of a grazing herd and start shooting.

A good hunter could shoot one hundred or more buffalo in a morning, then he would call his skinning crew to come up with the wagons. Hides were staked out on the prairie to dry. A well-cured hide was worth from $2.75 to $4, and many hunters earned more than $100 a day.

Soon the area between the Arkansas and Platte rivers was full of buffalo hunters who killed the great beasts and staked their hides out to cure and dry in the sun. Big bonfires were kept burning all night, and the slaughter went on twenty-four hours a day.

Soon the prairies were littered with the bleached bones of dead buffalo. These could be sold, too, for the manufacture of fertilizer and bone china. Settlers going to town would load their wagons with bones and collect as much as $14 a ton at the railroad stations. Some 32,000,-000 pounds of buffalo bones were shipped east from 1872 to 1874.

In 1867, when the railroad first crossed the plains of Nebraska and Kansas, trains were often held up for hours while herds of buffalo crossed the tracks.

Many Americans were sickened by this dreadful slaughter, and efforts were made in Congress and in state legislatures to put a stop to it. The railroads used their influence to help defeat these proposals. They alone knew how many hides were going to market, and this information was a closely kept secret. Not until after the buffalo were almost all gone, in the late 1880's, did the Santa Fe admit that it had carried 5,860,000 hides, valued at more than $40,000,000, out of Kansas.

Passengers on the early trains could see large herds of buffalo, deer, and antelope grazing calmly beside the tracks. They would open the car windows and shoot at the herds as the train sped along.

Sometimes a train would find its way blocked by a herd of buffalo. The engineer would not always dare to blow his whistle or try to force the train through, for stampeding buffalo could knock the cars from the tracks.

A correspondent for Frank Leslie's *Illustrated Newspaper* told of an encounter between a Kansas Pacific train and a stampeding herd. "In the dark of the evening the great mass of animals could scarcely be distinguished from the prairie itself save for the flash of gunfire," he wrote. "A little in advance of the engine they closed with the track and ran into the fire of 200 guns. It was a race for life."

Prairie fires were another menace for early-day trains. Such fires were usually started by the sparks from

A herd of buffalo, sighted near the tracks, is fired upon by passengers.

wood-burning locomotives, but occasionally Indians would set fire to the dry grass in the hope of getting revenge on the iron horse for invading their hunting grounds.

The Sioux and Cheyenne did their best to keep railroads out of the buffalo country, but they could not figure out a way to attack a train. They found that a locomotive was not hurt when they dashed up to it on their ponies and shot arrows or hurled lances at it. As soon as they had rifles, they tried riding alongside the cars and shooting into them, but this was not very effective either. The cars had double walls, and rail-

roadmen filled the hollow spaces with sand to stop the Indian bullets.

In Kansas, a Cheyenne chief thought he knew how the iron horse could be tamed. He organized his braves into two bands of about fifty men each, and stationed them on opposite sides of the Kansas Pacific track with a rawhide rope stretched between them. Soon a train came puffing along. When the engineer saw the Indians he opened his throttle wide, blew his whistle, and raced along at top speed. The cowcatcher hit the taut rope, and the Indians hanging onto it went flying. Several were killed, and many were injured.

On August 6, 1867, another Cheyenne band raided the Union Pacific tracks along the Platte River. One of the Indians, known as Porcupine, told years later how the red men had talked it over and decided:

"In these big wagons that go on this metal road, there must be things that are valuable—perhaps clothing. If we could throw these wagons off the iron they run on and break them open, we should find what was in them and take whatever might be useful to us."

"Once at the tracks," said Porcupine, "we got a big stick, and just before sundown tied it to the rails and sat down to watch and see what would happen."

The "big stick" was a railroad tie and the Indians had torn down a length of telegraph wire to lash it to the rails. When the telegraph went dead between Plum Creek and Willow Island, a repair crew led by William Thompson took out a handcar to find the break and repair it.

Porcupine and his companions waited patiently for a train to appear. Soon they saw "a small thing coming with something on it that moved up and down." It was Thompson and his five men, pumping their handcar. The little car hit the tie on the track, bounced off, and rolled down an embankment. The six men went sprawling. When they saw the Indians, they ran. The Cheyenne had horses, and soon all of the repair crew except Thompson had been run down, caught, and ruthlessly killed.

This pile of buffalo hides at Dodge City's railroad station in 1874 tells of the widespread slaughter of the buffalo. Dodge City alone shipped 1,500 hides a day in the 1870's. In an eighteen-year period, 12,000,000 buffalo were killed.

The Indians feared the arrival of the railroad in their western territory.

An Indian chasing Thompson shot him through the right arm, knocked him down with the butt of his rifle, leaped on him, and stabbed him in the neck. Thinking his victim was dead, the Indian then scalped Thompson. The white man was conscious and wanted to cry out in pain, but he managed to keep silent and did not move. "It felt as if the whole top of my head was taken off," he later told an Omaha newspaper reporter.

With a loud war whoop, the Indian jumped on his horse and galloped back on the track. On the way, the scalp slipped from his belt and fell to the ground.

Thompson hid in a clump of brush and watched the Indians pry up the rails and pile more ties on the track. Soon a westbound train came along, loaded with freight for Ogallala. The

engineer, "Bully" Brookes Bowers, saw the blockade and tried to break through it at twenty-five miles an hour, but the engine and five cars

Cheyenne Indians attack a railroad construction crew in an attempt to prevent the Iron Horse from crossing Kansas.

76

left the rails and upset. Bowers and his fireman were killed, and scattered coals from the firebox set fire to the wreckage.

Back in the caboose, Conductor William Kinney, his two brakemen, and a passenger saw the Indians coming. They took off as fast as they could run down the track, knowing that a second train was due soon and hoping to flag it down before the Indians caught them. Soon they could see the headlight of the approaching locomotive and hear the engineer whistle the signal for his crew to set the brakes.

With the Indians close behind, the four sprinted on, waving their lan-

terns. When they were outlined in the glare of the headlight, the Cheyennes dropped back. The panting white men were hauled up to the cab, and the engineer threw his train in reverse and retreated to Plum Creek.

Back at the wreck, Thompson watched from his hiding place in horror as the Indians scalped the dead engineer and threw his body on the flames. Then they broke into the boxcars, taking out whiskey, calico, and clothing. They drank the liquor, put on the clothes, and danced merrily around the burning wreckage for an hour. Then they galloped away.

A passenger train from Omaha is attacked on the Great Plains by a war party of Sioux.

Thompson, in great pain but still able to walk, hunted around until he found his scalp. Picking it up, he headed west along the tracks, and next morning staggered into Willow Island, his scalp in his hand.

The scalp was put in a bucket of water to keep it moist. Back at a hospital in Omaha, Dr. R. C. Moore tried to stitch it back on to Thompson's head. But it would not heal in place. So Thompson gave the scalp to the doctor for a souvenir.

As iron rails spread over the prairies, the savage Indians gradu-

ally retreated to new hunting grounds. But the railroads brought with them white men whose behavior was almost as wild and lawless as the red men who had moved on. These were the cowboys and gamblers and gunslingers who lived by the law of the six-shooter in cowtowns that sprang up along the tracks of the Kansas Pacific and the Santa Fe.

The first of these Wild West towns reached by the Kansas Pacific in 1867 was Abilene. This was the first railroad station within reach of the great longhorn cattle grazing grounds in east Texas. The Texas cattlemen began driving their herds up the famous Chisholm Trail.

The long, hot, dusty drive from Texas, across the Red River and up through Oklahoma and Kansas ended at Abilene. By the time the cowboys had their herds safely inside the loading corrals beside the railroad, they were ready to celebrate. And Abilene was ready for them. At the height of its glory, Abilene's main street had twenty saloons, twenty gambling joints, and ten dance halls.

As farmers and sheepherders moved west, they built barbed-wire fences to protect their land. The Texans were forced to take their herds farther west, too, and new trail towns were built to receive them. Most of these towns had no laws, or marshals to enforce them; cowboys who were slow on the draw died young. The trains ran east loaded with Texas longhorns for the Chicago meat packers, and ran back again loaded with whiskey, guns, gamblers, and dance hall girls.

Ellsworth and Wichita started as cow towns. Newton, Kansas, became known as "Shootin' Newton" because nine men died there in gun duels on a single night. Hunnewell had a bad reputation with railroaders, because drunken cowboys amused themselves by shooting out the locomotive headlight and taillights of the caboose. Lanterns in the hands of brakemen and conductors also made fine targets. Trainmen learned to put out the lights before arriving at Hunnewell.

All the Kansas trail towns were mild compared to Dodge City. From this wide-open and rip-roaring "queen of the cow towns," the Santa Fe shipped more than three thousand carloads of cattle a year from 1875 to 1885. The cattle drives started in the spring and lasted through August, and as many as two thousand Texas cowboys would whoop it up in a single season in Dodge.

The Texans did not like peace officers, and shot a few of them, and ran others out of town. Some of the Dodge City businessmen did not want law and order to come, feeling it was bad for business. Other members of the town council argued that the lives of respectable citizens were in danger with bullets flying around the streets. Finally the council telegraphed an invitation to Wyatt Earp, the celebrated gunfighter, to come to Dodge City and take on the job of marshal.

Earp established a line bounded by the Santa Fe railroad tracks running through Dodge. North of this line, he said, anyone caught wearing a gun would be shot on sight, or at least "buffaloed" and dragged off to jail. South of the tracks, however, almost anything short of a mass slaughter was allowed.

Many of the most famous frontier characters of the West took part in

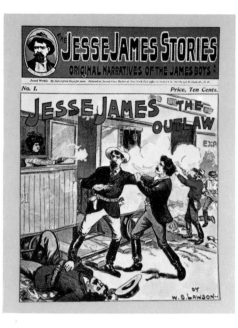

Turn-of-the-century dime novels were often based on Western themes. The James Boys were favorite characters.

the lively history of Dodge City. The quick-shooting dentist, Doc Holliday, and his girl friend, Big Nose Kate Fisher, lived there. The mayor of the town for several years was James H. "Hound Dog" Kelley, a saloonkeeper, whose hobby was raising pedigreed greyhounds and wolfhounds, and using them to hunt wolves and antelope.

William Barclay "Bat" Masterson came to Dodge as a youth of nineteen to work for a railroad grading contractor. When the job was done, Masterson's employer left town without paying him $300.

One day Bat heard that his ex-boss would be going through Dodge City the next day. When the train arrived, Bat climbed aboard, pistol in hand, and collected his $300.

Masterson later served as sheriff of Ford County, Kansas. He wore a pearl-grey derby and carried a gold-headed cane. It is said he got his nickname from his vigorous custom of using the cane to "bat" bad men into submission.

In 1879, the Santa Fe had an argument with the Denver & Rio Grande Railroad over which company had the right to build tracks through Colorado's Royal Gorge. Not all the fighting took place in the law courts. The Santa Fe hired Masterson and an army of thirty gunslingers, including Doc Holliday, to see that it got its way.

Bat and his men took a train to Canyon City, Colorado, where they met the Rio Grande's defenders. There was a great deal of shooting, but only one man was hit. Henry Jenkins, a Santa Fe partisan, was wounded in the rear as he was climbing out of a depot window.

Nobody knows for certain just who committed the first train robbery in America, but the first to make a profession of it were members of the notorious Reno gang. In 1866, the four Reno brothers and their associates climbed aboard an Ohio & Mississippi Railway train at Seymour, Indiana. As soon as the train was well on its way again they put on their masks, drew their pistols, and walked into the baggage coach ahead. The surprised guard opened his safe and handed over $13,000. Then the Reno boys pulled the cord

Mexican rancheros, Chinese laborers, American miners, and gamblers met in the saloons of San Francisco in the early days of the railroads' westward expansion.

to signal the engineer to stop, and as the train slowed down they calmly hopped off and disappeared.

The next year, when the same thing happened to the same train in the same place, there was great indignation in Indiana. The authorities had a good idea who was responsible for these outrages, and the four Reno brothers were rounded up and clapped in jail. They soon escaped, rejoined their gang, and held up a Jefferson, Madison & Indianapolis train, killing the express messenger and escaping with $96,000.

After two more holdups, five members of the gang were arrested and sent back by train to Seymour to stand trial. But they never arrived. Vigilantes stopped the train outside of Seymour, removed the Renos, and hanged them from trees beside the tracks.

As the years passed, the public began to lose its admiration for the railroads. Farmers in the Plains states thought freight rates were too high, and that railroads were charging too much money for the land the federal government had given them.

Cowboys drove their cattle from Texas up to the railroads in Kansas.

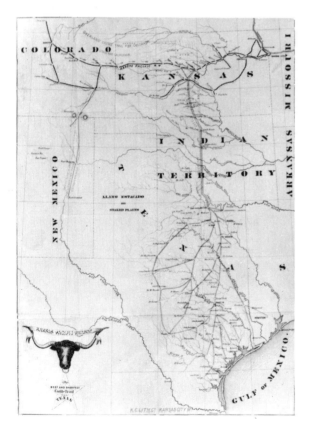

Some of these people were so bitter they did not consider train robbery a crime at all.

It was this attitude that helped Jesse James to carry on his career for eight years while an army of Pinkerton detectives, hired by the railroads, tried in vain to arrest him. Many people in Missouri knew where Jesse and his brother Frank were hiding, but the police could not find them.

The James boys robbed their first train near Adair, Iowa, in 1873. They removed a section of rail from the track just as a Chicago, Rock Island & Pacific passenger train

The Chisholm and Ellsworth trails led from Texas to Abilene, Dodge City, and other cowtowns on the Kansas Pacific.

came thundering along at full throttle. The engineer saw the gap and threw his locomotive into reverse. It was too late. The engine tipped over, crushing the engineer. Frank and Jesse calmly took $4,000 from the express-car safe, and a sackful of watches, rings, and currency from the passengers. Then they mounted their horses and rode away.

After several more successful train robberies, some staged with the help of Cole Younger and his brothers, Jesse James made his first mistake. He decided to branch out a little and see what success he might have in robbing banks.

When the James gang raided the First National Bank at Northfield, Minnesota, the townspeople grabbed their rifles and opened fire. Frank and Jesse escaped, but three members of the gang were shot dead, and Cole, Bob, and Jim Younger were wounded and captured.

After this the James brothers went into retirement for three years. Then they organized a new gang and resumed the robbing of trains, leaving banks strictly alone.

Finally, in 1882, the railroads persuaded Governor Crittenden of Missouri to offer a reward of $10,000 for Jesse's capture, dead or alive.

Cattle are driven up a chute into a Kansas Pacific stock car at Abilene.

SENSATIONAL AND STARTLING "HOLD UP" OF

This giant poster—measuring 12 by 20 feet—announced a popular play of 1896. It was based on the train robberies that plagued the Wild West, in the days after railroads had replaced stagecoaches as carriers of payroll money and the mails.

Frank and Jesse were living quite openly in a house in St. Joseph, Missouri, under the name of Howard. Other members of the gang also lived there, and on April 3, 1882,

one of them, Robert Ford, drew his revolver when Jesse was not looking—and shot him. Ford did not enjoy his reward, for everywhere he went he was shunned. The people sang a popular ballad about ". . . the dirty little coward who shot 'Mr. Howard,' and laid poor Jesse in his grave." At last people began to realize that outlaws such as the

Behind Frank (left) and Jesse James stand Cole and Bob Younger. The James Boys headed the most famous gang of train robbers ever to terrorize the Wild West.

James brothers were not at all like the legendary Robin Hood, who was said to have robbed the rich in order to give to the poor. For train robbers were just criminals, responsible for the deaths of a great many innocent railroad employees.

This change of heart was apparent

on March 13, 1912, when two desperadoes met the Southern Pacific's Sunset Express as it paused to take on water at a tank near Dryden, Texas. When one of them climbed into the express car, the Wells Fargo messenger, David A. Trousdale, was fortunately ready for him, and brained him with a mallet. Trousdale then picked up the dead man's rifle and killed the second robber, who was waiting outside of the express car to receive the stolen mail sacks and money.

Trousdale was warmly praised for his action, and Congress voted him a $1,000 reward for his courage. Times had changed.

Law enforcement officers like Wyatt Earp, seated second from left, and Bat Masterson, standing far right, were the men who broke the power of the gangsters in the West.

W.H. Harris.   Luke Short.   Bat Masterson
Charley Bassett.   Wyatt Earp.   M.F. McLean.   Neal Brown

RAILROADS AND FARMERS

A good way to get rich in a hurry in the years just before and after the Civil War was to start a new railroad in the West.

The typical railroad promoter would begin by finding a city that did not yet have a railroad, and was very anxious to have one. He would organize a company with the purpose of laying railway tracks from this city to another, hundreds or perhaps thousands of miles away.

Once the company was formed, the promoter would go to Congress or the state legislature to get a charter, a loan of public funds, and land grants. It was customary in the years after 1850 for the federal government to give huge tracts of free land in the Western states to railroad companies. As a general rule, these gifts amounted to six square miles of land for every mile of track which was built.

After the railroad was built this land could be sold to new settlers. In the meantime, railroad promoters would show brightly colored maps of their land holdings to wealthy people in the eastern United States and in Europe. Since it owned such vast tracts, the promoter would argue, the railroad could not help but become prosperous.

Unfortunately, many people who bought stocks and bonds in the new railroads lost all their investment. Even though the railroads were busy and earned a lot of money, little of this found its way back to

When buffalo-hunting Indians set the prairies ablaze, wooden coaches might be doused with water, so that trains could dash through the flames.

the pockets of the investors. Most of it seemed to go to the promoters.

The federal government from 1850 to 1871 passed out free land to railroad companies with a generous hand. The total has been listed at 131,000,000 acres, or more than the combined areas of New York, Pennsylvania, Ohio, and Indiana.

At the time Congress made its first land grants in 1850 to aid the construction of railroads in Illinois, Mississippi, and Alabama, the government had been trying for years to sell land to settlers in these states at $1.25 an acre. There had been few takers. But after giving the railroads half the land on either side of the tracks in six-mile strips, the government found it could sell the remaining land at $2.50 an acre. So the public really lost nothing.

"We are met," said Senator William R. King, during a congressional debate in 1850 concerning a land grant of 2,595,000 acres for the Illinois Central Railroad, "by the objection that this is an immense grant—that it is a great quantity of land. Well, sir; it is a great quantity, but it will be there for five hundred years; and unless some mode of the kind proposed be adopted," he continued, "it will never command ten cents."

What the Senator said was true. There was, indeed, "a great quantity" of public land being given away free to private companies. But the land was not helping the public if it lay there, unproductive.

The railroads, with their many millions of acres of land to sell, did everything they could to encourage westward movement between 1870 and 1900. Much of the credit for the swift development of the West belongs to the western railroads, who sent their agents to Europe to round up new settlers.

It was not hard to persuade the Europeans to leave their old homes.

Immigrants traveling west set up housekeeping and spent their entire journey in railway coaches like this one. Railroad men often spoke of them as "Zulu cars."

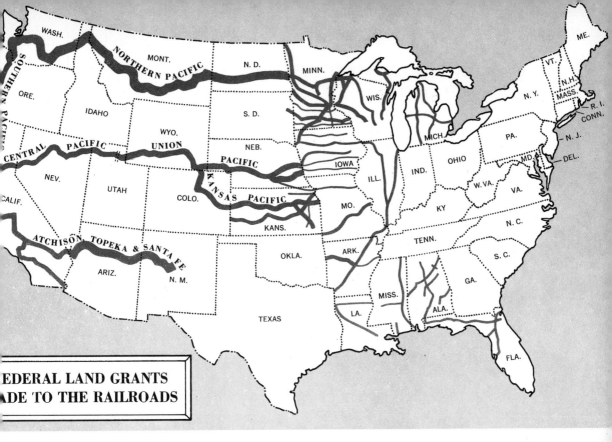

Approximate areas of federal land grants to the railroads are shown above. Railroads helped pay for their construction costs by selling these lands to farmers.

The wheat harvests had been poor in the 1870's, for example, and the peasants thought they would do better in America, where rich, new farmland could be bought from the railroads for a few dollars an acre.

The first railroad to receive a big federal land grant, the Illinois Central, carried out the first large-scale job of transplanting settlers to the empty prairie.

Into the rocky fields of New England went the IC's agents, telling of how a farmer could plow a straight furrow for miles in Illinois and never hit a root or a stone. Railroad orators visited every county fair in the eastern states, offering free

This Union Pacific locomotive—one of the first to pull "Zulu cars" of immigrants—was photographed in 1869.

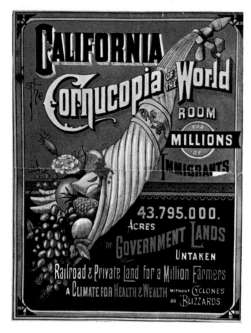

Posters drew settlers into the West

transportation and other extras to new settlers. These efforts were highly successful. So many people left Vermont that land prices dropped forty per cent.

The IC agents were busy in Europe, too. Its missionaries to Norway and Sweden sent back streams of new colonists to Illinois. By 1861, the railroad had sold 1,500,000 acres of its land and the population of the state doubled in eleven years.

Other western railroads followed the lead of the Illinois Central. Salesmen in Europe spoke of the fertile soil, tall grass, and sweet water to be had almost for the taking along the tracks of the Northern Pacific, Great Northern, Union Pacific, the Burlington, and the Santa Fe.

C. B. Schmidt, a very successful land agent for the Santa Fe railway, visited a colony of wealthy Mennonites—descendants of German farmers who had settled in Russia in 1786. They were not happy about life under the Czar, and listened with interest to Schmidt's description of the great state of Kansas.

When the Russian government discovered what Schmidt was trying to do, czarist police were sent to run him out of the country. He dodged them, rounded up two thousand Mennonites and all their worldly goods, and loaded them aboard a

Railroads and steamship lines advertised in Europe to bring farmers to America.

In the center of this lithograph stands the heroic figure of a Granger. Farmers found protection from the powerful railroads in the Grange organization.

steamer. They arrived in Kansas with $2,200,000 in gold sewed into the linings of their coats and dresses. The Santa Fe was so delighted to see them that it offered to haul building materials free for them for one year.

Jim Hill's Northern Pacific and

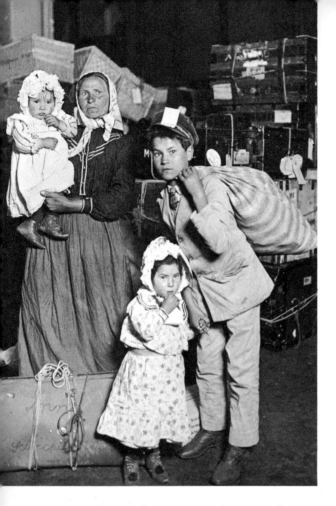

This newly arrived Italian family was photographed on Ellis Island in 1905.

Great Northern railroads settled Minnesota, the Dakotas, Montana, and the Pacific Northwest with the Swedes and Norwegians who did not mind the cold winters.

Unfortunately, the settlers did not always find life in the American West as rosy as the land agents described it. Nobody had mentioned the tornadoes, cloudbursts, frosts, droughts, and plagues of locusts.

And frequently farmers who overcame these hardships found that the railroads, like Nature, had an un-

friendly side. Farmers began to complain about the freight rates they had to pay to get their produce hauled to market.

There were good reasons for such complaints. In the 1870's, many a state was served by a single railroad; the company could charge very high freight rates and no one could do anything about it. One year, corn that sold for a dollar a bushel in New York would bring only fifteen cents to the farmer in Iowa. It was cheaper to burn this corn in farmhouse stoves to keep warm than to sell it and buy coal or wood.

Later on, when more railroads were built, a new evil appeared. Rates went down as competition appeared, but now the farmers suffered under the rebate system, in which large shippers would receive lower rates than those paid by small customers without influence.

To fight for fair treatment, midwest farmers banded together in the National Grange of the Patrons of Husbandry, more often known simply as The Grange. The united farmers were able to elect their own representatives to state legislatures, and several states passed laws requiring the railroads to treat all their customers alike.

The railroads fought back, hiring lawyers to attack the so-called "Granger laws" in the courts. Finally the United States Supreme Court handed down an important decision which said state legislatures had no control over the rates charged by railroads which operated in two or more states.

This meant that the "Granger laws" were worthless, so the farmers took their complaints to Congress. A congressional investigating committee proved that the railroads had been guilty of many dishonest practices, including the bribing of judges and state officers.

Congress was shaken by these findings, and in 1887, it created the Interstate Commerce Commission, with power to regulate railroad freight and passenger rates.

Now the ICC has strong controls over freight rates, passenger fares, and operating practices of all kinds of common carriers—railroads, buses, trucks, and river barges—which operate across state lines.

In 1873, this cartoon, called The Grange Awakening the Sleepers, *made use of a pun on the old-fashioned word for cross-ties, or "sleepers." The Grange, pitchfork in hand, is arousing the public to the "bribery" and "extortion" of the railroads.*

Grasshopper plagues such as this one, photographed in Nebraska in 1874, were hazards of life in the West which railroad land-grant posters never mentioned.

The accident pictured here occurred on the Western Maryland Railroad in 1863.

WRECKS AND INVENTIONS

Train wrecks were very common in the early days of American railroading. As long as the cars rolled along at no more than fifteen or twenty miles an hour, these incidents were seldom serious. But as locomotives became bigger and faster, collisions and derailments killed many hundreds of passengers and trainmen.

In the winter of 1876, two locomotives were pulling the New York Central's Pacific Express across a bridge at Ashtabula, Ohio, when suddenly it seemed to the engineer of the leading locomotive that he was going uphill. He was, for the bridge was sagging in the middle under the heavy load. Quickly he opened his throttle, and his engine broke away from the rest of the train and leaped to safety. Eleven cars and the other engine plunged 150 feet to the frozen creek bed. The heating stoves in the cars scattered hot coals over the wreckage, and eighty-three persons died in the blazing wreckage.

The same thing happened in 1887 to a fifteen-car train bound for Niagara Falls on the tracks of the Toledo, Peoria & Western Railroad. This time, eighty-two passengers died. Again in 1887, forty people died and one hundred and twenty were hurt when a Boston & Providence train went through a wooden bridge at Forest Hills, near Boston.

Still another famous wreck was blamed on the difference in the widths of track of two connecting railroads, the New York Central and the Lake Shore & Michigan Southern. The rails of the Central's track were the standard four feet, eight and one-half inches apart, but the Lake Shore width, or gauge, was four feet ten inches. This led to the use of "compromise cars," with wheels spaced just far enough apart to fit the Lake Shore track.

One December night near Angola, New York, a wheel on a "compromise car" at the tail end of the New York Express slipped off the track. The car bumped along the ties for a few hundred yards and then, as the train was crossing a bridge, broke loose and tumbled to the bottom of a ravine.

The next car was derailed and it, too, broke its coupling and plunged off the bridge. Both cars burst into flames, set on fire by hot coals spill-ed from their heating stoves. When the engineer looked back and saw two cars were missing, and the flames in the canyon, he stopped the train and backed up. The crew broke the ice in Big Sisters Creek and threw water on the fires—too late to save forty-nine passengers.

Wrecks such as these forced the railroads to strengthen bridges and to build steel cars heated by steam from the locomotives. The "Angola Horror" put an end to "compromise cars" and hastened the building of tracks of a standard width.

In the early days, tracks had been made of wood covered with thin straps of iron. Often a rail would break and poke through the bottom of a passing car. These broken rails, or "snake heads," as they were call-ed, caused many fatal accidents.

Modern all-metal T-shaped rails and the hook-headed spikes that hold them down were designed by Robert L. Stevens, president of the Camden & Amboy, while he was on his way to England in 1830 to buy equipment for his new line.

By the time of the Civil War almost all United States railroads were using solid iron rails of Stevens' design, but in England, something new had been invented. An iron-master named Henry Bessemer found that if air were blown through a vat of molten iron, some of the carbon would be burned out of it and the result would be a much stronger metal—steel.

Other countries had their railroad disasters, too. In this wreck in 1842, at Meudon, France, fifty-seven persons died after an engine snapped an axle.

In 1863, the Pennsylvania Railroad bought some rails made of Bessemer's steel. Unlike iron, they did not bend or wear out under heavy loads. Soon rolling mills were turning out steel rails, and by 1900, iron rails had disappeared.

Because steel expands when it is warm, tracklayers leave a little gap between the end of two rails which butt together. In very cold weather this gap may be as much as a quarter of an inch, but when the temperature is one hundred degrees the gap will close. The rhythmic "clickety-clack" of a train rolling over these rail joints may sound pleasant to a passenger, but to a railroadman it is a costly nuisance. Each click means a tiny bit of steel has chipped off the end of the rail, hastening the day when it must be replaced.

In 1933, the Delaware & Hudson Railroad tried welding the ends of rails together as they were laid, eliminating the gaps. Many railroaders thought this would not work. They were sure the tracks would buckle and warp in hot summer weather, but they were wrong. The great holding power of the spikes, ties, and ballast kept the rails in line. Many railroads now use these long "ribbon" rails. Passengers may roll as far as six miles before they hear a click.

The invention of the telegraph by Samuel F. B. Morse in 1844 was another forward step in railroading safety and efficiency. With it, a station agent could learn the exact location of every train along the main line, and assure locomotive engineers that there was no danger of a head-on collision — or "cornfield

98

meet"—as they hurried on their way to the next station.

The first use of telegraphic train orders came in 1851 when Charles Minot, superintendent of the Erie Railroad, was riding on a train going west, bound for Port Jervis, New York. Following the orders in his timetable, the engineer sidetracked the train at Harriman (then known as Turner's), New York, to let an eastbound train pass. When the other train did not appear, Minot grew fidgety.

Finally he asked the operator of the local telegraph line to find out if the eastbound train had arrived at Goshen, the next station fourteen miles west of Harriman. Back over the wire clicked the answer: "No." So Minot sent another message: "To operator at Goshen: Hold eastbound train until further orders. Charles Minot, Supt. Erie."

Then the superintendent ordered his train crew to go ahead to Goshen. The engineer balked. He did not trust the strange clicking noises carried over a slender copper wire. So Minot took the throttle himself.

At Goshen there still was no sign of the tardy train. More telegraph messages were exchanged with the next station, and again Minot's train rolled westward "against the time cards." This went on until the train finally arrived safely at Port Jervis, saving many hours of useless delay.

Some railroads were slow to adopt the telegraph. A terrible wreck at Revere, Massachusetts, occurred because the Eastern Railroad, of Massachusetts, as late as 1871, still used the old-fashioned timetable system.

On a hot summer night, the express train for Portland, Maine, pulled out of Boston depot, when the timetable said it should. Up ahead, however, other trains were not on time. A local train, two hours behind schedule, was unloading passengers at Revere when the Portland Express came charging along, its engineer confident that he had a clear track ahead. The express train made kindling wood of the local's cars, and twenty-nine passengers were killed.

The people of Massachusetts were outraged, and no one can blame them. This was 1871, and the telegraph had been in use for a quarter of a century. The railroad president was forced to resign, and a new train superintendent who understood the uses of telegraphy was hired.

Some early locomotives had brakes operated by steam pressure, but many of the high-wheeled passenger engines built as late as 1880 could be stopped in a hurry only by throwing them into reverse and spinning the drivers. If an engineer wanted to slow down his train he would blow a whistle signal, and brakemen would scramble from car to car, setting the hand brakes.

On freight cars the brake wheels were mounted on the roofs, and many a brakeman fell to his death on a stormy winter night trying to walk the icy, treacherous "running boards."

A piece of early railroad equipment which was responsible for the death or injury of many brakemen was the old link-and-pin coupler used to fasten one car to another. To work it, a brakeman had to stand between the cars. If he did not get the pin into the link at the right moment, the cars would come together with a bang and crush him.

In 1868, a veteran of the Confederate Army, Major Eli H. Janney, invented a clever new device to hold railroad cars together. He called it a "knuckle" coupler, because it looked much like a human hand with the fingers curled. When two cars "shake hands" with Janney's couplers, the brakeman stands safely at the side and controls them with a long lever.

The very next year a young veteran of the Union Army invented the air brake, a device which was to save the lives of many railroad employees and passengers. When George Westinghouse came to New York after the Civil War he was shocked by the dreadful loss of life in a head-on collision between two trains near Schenectady. The engineers had seen each other coming, but they could not stop.

Many people scoffed at the idea of halting a speeding train with invisible air, but Westinghouse proved that it would work with a demonstration on a train running between Pittsburgh and Steubenville, Ohio. He put an air pump and tank on the locomotive, and ran an air pipe from car to car, leading to a piston and cylinder connected to the brakes on each. When the engineer

Conductors were often responsible for the safety of the whole train; the signal lanterns these men hold were vital safety equipment in 1864.

By 1885, *when this print was made, railroads required the specialized work of yardmen, switchmen, signalmen, brakemen, baggage masters, and others.*

opened a valve, compressed air flowed through the pipe and set all the brakes.

The system had one serious fault. If there were any leaks in the pipeline, the air pressure would be lost and the brakes would not work. So Westinghouse changed the system around. He put an air tank on each car, which made pressure available in the connecting air lines at all times. Nowadays when an engineer wants to stop, he lets a little pressure out of the lines and the air in each car tank sets the brakes on that car.

The engineer has always been regarded as the man with the most interesting and romantic job in railroading. Many youngsters now hope to grow up to be jet pilots, or spacemen, but when our grandfathers were small boys the locomotive engineer was their hero.

How they envied him, sitting like a king on his high throne on the right-hand side of the cab! His hand was steady on the throttle, and his keen eyes scanned the track ahead as the Fast Mail thundered through the countryside. He always waved to the admiring children and the pretty girls who stood by the track to watch the train go past, and sometimes he would sound a mighty blast on his whistle, frightening the

horses and cows and making echoes rumble through the hills.

The left-hand seat in the engine cab belonged to the fireman, but he seldom sat on it. He was too busy shoveling coal or pitching cordwood into the firebox, to make sure the engineer had plenty of steam.

Even going downhill the fireman got little rest. When the engineer gave the signal it was his job to pick up a pot of mutton tallow, crawl out the cab window onto the locomotive running boards, and edge along the hot boiler to the cylinders. Here he would pour some of the tallow into the steam chest to lubricate the valves. This was an uncomfortable and dangerous duty, especially on a stormy night. But the "tallowpot" who did his work well and without complaint could expect to be promoted to the right-hand seat and be admired as a brave engineer.

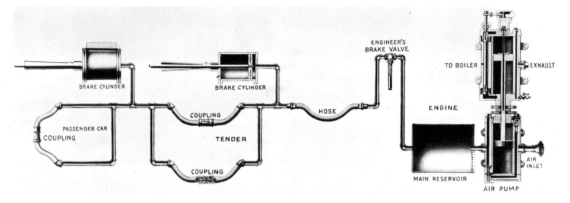

The Westinghouse non-automatic, straight-air brake was developed in 1869.

Today the fireman has a comfortable chair behind the windshield in the snug cab of a diesel engine, and he no longer has to tend a fire, or watch the water level in a boiler.

The conductor's job does not seem very glamorous, but he is the real boss of the passenger train. The engineer does not take the train out of the station until the conductor gives him the "highball," and when the train stops for any reason on the main line, the conductor orders a brakeman out to warn other trains by placing flares on the track a safe distance ahead and behind.

In the old days it was difficult for a conductor riding in a caboose at the end of a long string of freight cars to give orders to the engineer at the head end. A conductor named Ayres on the Erie Railroad was first to solve this problem.

He bought a ball of twine, and threaded it through staples along the car roofs from the caboose to the engine cab, where he tied it to a piece of wood. Then, according to railway historian Stewart Holbrook, he told the engineer:

"When that hunk of wood hops off the floor, you will know I want you to start or stop, whichever we ain't doing when it hops."

Using radiotelephones, engineers now can talk to their conductors back in the cabooses. These radios sometimes come in handy for other purposes, too. On a windy day in February, 1959, a group of Sea Explorer Scouts capsized their sailboat in the rough Columbia River near Vancouver, Washington. The engineer of a passing freight train saw the accident and radioed his dis-

Janney's automatic "knuckle" coupler was safer to use than the "link-and-pin" system shown on the facing page.

Westinghouse's brake was put to the test in 1869 when a farmer's wagon stalled on the tracks near Pittsburgh and made it necessary to use the brake quickly. It worked.

patcher to call the Coast Guard. A boat arrived in time to save all but one of the boys from drowning.

With the development of short-wave radios and signaling devices built into locomotive cabs, many railroads with heavy traffic have adopted the new centralized traffic control system. CTC makes it possible for a single dispatcher to con-

The "link-and-pin" coupler was dangerous.

Brakemen were often crushed by the cars.

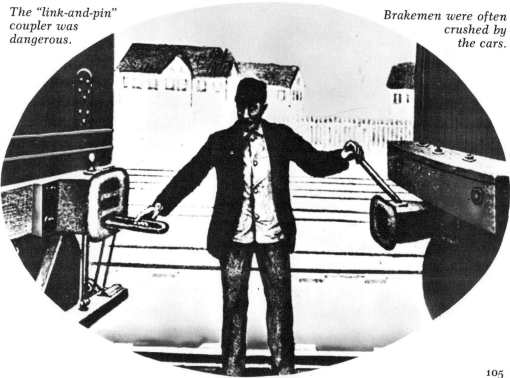

Trains rushing toward each other in the night had only their own whistles and signalmen (left) to give them warning.

trol the movements of many trains on hundreds of miles of railroad track. On a board before him is a model of the trackage. Colored lights show him the location of every train. By throwing toggle switches on the control board, he can open or close track switches anywhere on his division to put trains onto sidings.

All these improvements have made the job of a railroadman easier and safer. No longer do life insurance companies list railroading as an extra-hazardous occupation, and seldom do we hear such tragic and heroic stories as that of Engineer Edward Kennar of the New York Central Railroad.

One dark rainy night, in 1887, near Batavia, New York, Kennar was at the throttle of an eastbound train when he saw a landslide on the track ahead. It was too late to stop, and the engine hit the pile of rocks and mud and toppled down an embankment, pinning Kennar in the wreckage. As the other trainmen tried to pull the dying engineer loose, he opened his eyes and with his last breath gasped out: "Flag Number Five."

In their excitement, the train crew had forgotten that No. 5, a westbound train, was due any minute on the other track. Off they ran,

their lanterns bobbing, and flagged it down in time to prevent another wreck.

The throttle was taken from the cab of Kennar's wrecked engine and plated with silver. For many years

HE DANGER SIGNAL.

it hung on the wall of the meeting room of Division 46 of the Brotherhood of Locomotive Engineers at Albany as a memorial to a brave railroadman who stayed with his engine when he saw danger ahead, and whose last thought was for the safety of another train.

On September 1, 1894, a forest fire swept over three counties in eastern Minnesota, destroying several towns and taking 418 lives. When south-

This disaster in Rhode Island in 1853 was the first train wreck ever photographed.

bound Limited Train No. 4 of the St. Paul & Duluth Railroad pulled into Hinckley, Minnesota, at 4 P.M. on this terrible day, engineer James Root found the outskirts of the town already blazing, and a crowd of two hundred frightened people waiting at the depot for the train to take them to safety. They climbed aboard, and Root started on toward St. Paul, Minnesota.

Soon the engine ran into an impassable curtain of fire. With the engine cab and baggage car smoldering, he jammed on the brakes, and threw the locomotive in reverse.

Back through the doomed town went the train as the flames advanced toward the track. Soon even the ties were ablaze. Root's fireman dived into the water tank to escape flames spurting into the cab, then came out again to throw buckets of water over the engineer, whose denims were beginning to burn.

Inside the train a brave Negro porter, John W. Blair, tried to calm the panicky passengers. He made them lie down on the car floors when fierce heat shattered the windows and set the woodwork afire. He went up and down the train, pouring water on the heads and clothing of women and children.

At last the train reached Skunk Lake, a muddy pond six miles north of Hinckley. Root fell unconscious from his burns after he braked the train to a halt, but the grateful passengers carried him to safety in the nearby marsh.

The grateful survivors honored Blair at a party in St. Paul, and the railroad company gave the porter a fine gold watch for "gallant and faithful discharge of duty." The heroic engineer was bedridden for months from the burns he received while he stayed at his throttle.

Train accidents nowadays are rare. The Association of American Railroads calculates that the average passenger could have traveled over two billion miles in 1959 without a fatal mishap. No wonder American railroads can boast that their passenger trains now offer the safest form of travel in the world.

In December 1876 the Lake Shore & Michigan Southern's Pacific Express *plunged through a faulty Howe truss bridge at Ashtabula, Ohio, killing eighty-three people.*

STRIKES AND
BROTHERHOODS

In the early days of American railroading, there were few complaints about long hours and low wages. The railroads were struggling to prove their worth, and pioneer offi-cials were always ready to peel off their coats and pitch in alongside their employees when there was a job to be done.

As the years passed, this feeling

Trains like this crack New York Central express of 1884 required large crews to service and run them on tight schedules.

tion which could speak for them all, in dealings with their employers. They called it the Brotherhood of Locomotive Engineers, and it has become one of the strongest trade-unions in the nation.

Five years later the Order of Railway Conductors was formed. Next came the Brotherhood of Locomotive Firemen, organized in 1873, after a fireman was killed in a wreck and his friends were passing the hat to collect money for his widow.

The brotherhoods tried at first to settle peacefully their disagreements

The Brotherhood of Locomotive Engineers, the first railroad union, awarded certificates like these to members.

changed. Railroads came under the control of investors interested only in profits. In the 1850's, when railroads were beginning to earn a great deal of money, their owners cut wages and ordered their men to work longer shifts. Workers who dared to complain were fired.

A group of railroad engineers met in April, 1863, to form an organiza-

The Sixth Maryland militia fires on a hostile crowd of strikers and sympathizers near the Baltimore railroad station during the Baltimore and Ohio strike of 1877.

with the railroad owners. Then, in the summer of 1877, when six railroads announced new pay cuts, angry workers lost their patience.

Violence broke out at Martinsburg, West Virginia, where striking firemen and brakemen stopped all the Baltimore and Ohio freight trains. The railroad asked for the arrest of the strikers, but angry townspeople chased the police away. In two days seventy trains, with 1,200 loaded freight cars, were stalled at Martinsburg. President Rutherford B. Hayes sent federal troops to herd off the strikers at bayonet point, and the trains began running again.

By now the strike fever had spread all along the B & O system. More violence brought more calls for troops. At Camden Station, Baltimore, three companies of militia fought a bloody skirmish with a mob of 20,000 strike sympathizers. By the time the smoke drifted away, thirteen lay dead in the streets and one hundred more were wounded.

Pennsylvania Railroad trainmen now went on strike at Pittsburgh. A thousand federal troops arrived by train from Philadelphia to force them back to work. Rocks were thrown, and the soldiers opened fire. Twenty men were killed, and a woman and three children were among the wounded.

This sent the people of Pittsburgh into a black rage. A crowd of 15,000 advanced on the soldiers, and the outnumbered troops retreated hastily to the railroad roundhouse. Some of the townspeople had guns, too, and three soldiers trying to escape from the roundhouse were shot down.

Rioters broke into hardware stores, taking guns and ammunition. Shouting and cursing, the mob attacked all the Pennsylvania Railroad property they could find, burning the Union Depot and Hotel, the company's offices and repair shops, and destroying one hundred locomotives and five hundred cars. Finally the desperate soldiers broke out of the roundhouse, firing as they ran. They escaped to the nearby town of Sharpsburg, leaving twenty-three more dead behind them.

Now the federal government sent 10,000 more troops to the aid of the Pennsylvania Railroad. General Winfield Scott Hancock issued stern orders to the rioters: Behave or be shot. The first Pennsylvania train out of Pittsburgh pushed ahead of it a gondola car carrying a squad of soldiers and a Gatling gun.

There were other riots, and more killings, in Buffalo, Chicago, Boston, and Providence. In two weeks, more than a hundred people died, five hundred were injured, and millions of dollars worth of railroad property was destroyed. The strikes of 1877 were costly, bloody failures, and many of the strike leaders were put on the employers' black list so that no railroad would hire them.

Responsible union leaders saw that violence was not the answer to the problems of workingmen. The young secretary-treasurer of the Brotherhood of Locomotive Firemen, Eugene Victor Debs, said that workers who took part in the shooting, burning, and looting were guilty of "anarchy and revolution."

New brotherhoods were being formed: the Railway Trainmen in 1883, the Telegraphers in 1886, the Maintenance of Way Employees in 1887, and the Railway Carmen in 1891. These organizations were interested only in the needs of their own members. They would not stand together against the railroad owners. On the other hand, Debs noted with interest how the railroads always worked together in putting down labor uprisings.

Unable to persuade the brotherhoods to join forces, Debs in 1893 formed the new American Railway Union, open to all railroad workers, skilled and unskilled, from aristo-

Federal cavalry troops clear the way for a train to go through the A.R.U. strike lines during the Pullman strike of 1894.

cratic engineers down to the lowliest engine wiper. In a year he had signed up 150,000 members.

James J. Hill and his Great Northern Railway were the first to test the power of Debs and the ARU. The Great Northern had cut the wages of its workers three times in less than a year. By March, 1894, the pay for engineers and conductors had been whittled down to $80 a month. Ordinary roundhouse workers made ten cents an hour. Debs demanded a raise for his members, and Hill ignored him. At noon on April 13, Debs called a strike.

For eighteen days nothing moved on the Great Northern except mail trains. From St. Paul to Seattle, freight piled up on platforms. Passenger coaches stood silent and empty. At last Hill gave in. Wages were boosted an average of sixteen dollars a month. It was the first real victory for any railroad union in the United States.

Now Debs turned his attention to the little city of Pullman, Illinois, where George Mortimer Pullman had grown wealthy building Pullman sleeping cars. Debs had been critical of the Pullman Company's treatment of its workers. Mr. Pullman owned the town and everything in it. Pullman workers paid high rents to live in Pullman tenements. They bought food and clothing in Pullman stores, went to school and church in Pullman buildings, and even borrowed books—for a fee—from the Pullman library. Anyone who dared to criticize the company was fired instantly and his name placed on a black list.

In May, 1894, the company cut wages, but left rents at the same level. A committee of employees called on the management to protest. When the company stood firm, the workers held a meeting and voted overwhelmingly to strike.

ARU members voted to help Pullman strikers by refusing to handle any train with Pullman cars in them. This brought the railroads into the strike, too.

In spite of Debs' orders to avoid violence, mobs of strike sympathizers formed and halted trains on the Illinois Central and Panhandle lines. A federal court ordered the strikers to stop interfering with

Eugene Debs campaigns in 1912 for the United States Presidency on the Socialist ticket.

trains, but by now 100,000 railroad workers were on strike, and there was no holding them back.

Federal troops poured into Chicago to enforce the court orders. There were clashes between soldiers and strike sympathizers. Railroad properties were smashed and burned. Two men were killed on July 6, and on July 7, when national guardsmen escorting a train ran into a mob at 49th and Loomis streets; there was a brisk battle in which twenty rioters were slain.

The strike was broken. Trains ran again, the Pullman Company factory reopened, and every employee coming back to work was required to sign a "yellow dog" con-

tract—an agreement in which he promised not to join a labor union.

Debs and some of his followers were sentenced to six months in jail for contempt of court because they had ignored the court order to stop interfering with the movement of the mails. The sentence was appealed to the United States Supreme Court, but Debs lost, and he and his companions went to prison. While Debs was behind bars, the American Railway Union withered away.

The Pullman strike was a failure, but it helped to improve the lot of the American worker. As a result of it, an investigating commission appointed by President Cleveland wrote a report which became the foundation for modern labor laws. Today, when railroad companies and their workers disagree, federal mediation boards try to settle the disputes and prevent strikes.

The new method of peaceful arbitration has been very successful for the railroad workers. In 1935, the average railway employee earned only $31.70 a week. Now the average railroader's paycheck is well over one hundred dollars a week. If Debs were alive today, he would see that America has given its workingmen a square deal within the framework of the free enterprise system.

George M. Pullman

This cartoon criticized Debs' union as a threat to the nation's progress.

In the 1880's, passengers had to cram their way into depot lunch rooms to get food.

RIDING THE RAILS

Before the Civil War railroad travel was not very pleasant. Passengers were crowded into tiny, flat-roofed cars that were little more than boxes on wheels. They sat on hard wooden benches. Smoke and sparks, soot and dust poured through the open windows in summer. In winter passengers would huddle around wood stoves, shivering each time the conductor, going from car to car to collect tickets, opened the doors and let in blasts of icy air.

Complaints from customers soon forced the railroads to make their cars more comfortable. One of the first improvements was what was called a sleeping car, although only a very weary traveler could have slept in one.

In these cars, wooden bunks or shelves were stacked three deep against the wall. At first, there were no sheets, blankets, or pillows. The passenger was expected to cover himself with his coat.

The coming of George Mortimer Pullman's wonderful Pullman Pal-

As stopovers were short, slow eaters ran the risk of being left behind.

ace Car after the Civil War made it possible for the first time for railroads to carry passengers in dignity and comfort. In the middle of a sleepless night spent aboard a sleeping car between Buffalo, New York, and Westfield, Massachusetts, young Pullman had sketched a rough plan for a passenger coach with comfortable berths let down from the ceiling on ropes and pulleys.

Two cars rebuilt along the lines suggested by Pullman went into service in 1858 on the Chicago and Alton Railroad. Passengers liked them, so in 1864 Pullman was encouraged to risk his own funds in the construction of a radically new car. He called it the *Pioneer*, and before it was finished he had spent more than $20,000—four times the cost of any previous passenger car on any railroad.

The *Pioneer* had many unusual features. Its trucks were cushioned with blocks of solid rubber, to give it a smooth ride. In the daytime, the upper berths swung up against the ceiling, providing a place to store bedclothing. There were plush carpets, mirrors, and carved woodwork.

To make room for its hinged berths, the *Pioneer* was built a foot wider and two and a half feet higher

than any other railroad car of its day. This meant that it could not squeeze through some of the narrow bridges or get past the depot platforms on the Chicago & Alton. For a time the *Pioneer* seemed fated to sit idly on its sidetrack, beautiful but useless.

When, in April, 1865, the President of the United States was assassinated at Ford's Theater in Wash-ington, D.C., the North was plunged into deep mourning. Elaborate plans were made for a funeral train to bear the body of the martyred President back to his home at Springfield, Illinois.

It is said that Mrs. Abraham Lincoln, on a visit to Illinois a short time before, had seen and admired Pullman's handsome new passenger car. She asked that it be attached to the funeral train at Chicago for her personal use. So Chicago & Alton bridgebuilders and carpenters went hastily to work to widen the bridges and whittle down the station platforms so the *Pioneer* could pass.

Thousands of people saw Mrs. Lincoln riding in Pullman's new car. Later the Chicago and North Western Railroad made similar changes in bridge and depot clearances so the commander of the

This New York Central coach of 1858 was uncomfortable for night travel.

George Pullman's new sleeping car, the Pioneer, *was attached to Lincoln's funeral train; thousands of people saw it.*

Union armies, General Ulysses S. Grant, could make a triumphant trip home from Detroit to Galena, Illinois, in the *Pioneer.*

After this, everyone wanted to ride in a Pullman car. Pullman now organized the Pullman Palace Car Company, and began turning out

replicas of the *Pioneer* by the dozens. Soon they were rolling on railroads all over the United States and in Great Britain and Italy, too.

Where George M. Pullman made it possible for railroad passengers to sleep in comfort, Frederick H. Harvey let them eat without fear of food poisoning. "Hotel cars," which served meals while rolling along the tracks, had appeared on some eastern railroads in the early seventies, but hungry travelers in the west were obliged to wait until the train paused briefly at a station, and then dash out to a quick lunch counter to gulp down sandwiches and coffee while the impatient conductor paced the platform, watch in hand.

Sleeping cars of the 1850's were a small improvement over sitting up all night.

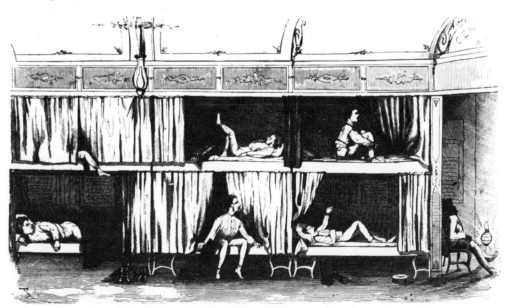

121

In the late nineteenth century, when traveling companies toured cities and towns with stage productions, America's popular actors and actresses were often seen on trains.

The food in depot lunch counters was always very bad, the prices high, and the service poor. Fred Harvey, a Kansas restaurant man, persuaded the Santa Fe Railroad in 1876 that it would be good business to give its passengers better treatment. With the company's assistance, he opened a lunchroom in the Topeka station. Customers were astonished to find the place clean and freshly painted, the food hot and tasty, and the waitresses neat and polite. There were even such luxuries as tablecloths and napkins.

By 1900, Fred Harvey and the railroad were partners in fifteen hotels, forty-seven restaurants, and a fleet of thirty dining cars.

Fred Harvey is best remembered for the famous "Harvey Girls." He wanted his waitresses to be pretty and ladylike, but it was not easy to find such girls in the rough western towns served by the Santa Fe. So Harvey advertised in eastern newspapers for "Young women of good character, attractive and intelligent, 18 to 30." The "Harvey Girls" all wore black dresses with bows, black shoes and stockings, and white hair ribbons. They earned $17.50 a month, plus room and board, and had to keep a strict 10 P.M. curfew.

There were always many more men than women along the Santa Fe line, so the pretty "Harvey Girls" always had plenty of beaux, and

Fred Harvey was kept busy finding replacements for those who found husbands. They seemed to prefer the company of railroadmen, and some 5,000 of them, according to Santa Fe historians, married engineers, conductors, and station agents —and helped tame the Wild West.

Another civilizing influence on rail travel was the appearance of the private car. Many a millionaire in the old days owned his own railway car, and had it attached to a passenger train when he wanted to take a trip.

Traveling artists sometimes lived in their own cars as they toured the country. Fritzi Scheff, Adelina Patti, and Edwin Booth kept private cars, equipped with kitchens, sleeping rooms, and baths. Miss Scheff was said to complain loudly when rough track caused the bath water to slosh over the side of her tub.

These luxurious cars are seldom seen on United States railroads today. The Pullman Company, which built some 350 private cars, turned out its last one in 1930, and during World War II most of those still in existence were turned over to the government for military purposes.

The first private car in the United States was built by the army for President Lincoln. It was used only once, to carry his coffin in his funeral train.

The Chicago & Alton used this lady to promote their new Palace chair cars.

Trains were accepted as safe transportation for the family—even for children.

Private Pullman cars were luxuriously decorated with rich carpets and mirrors.

Since that time, every President of the United States has had a private railroad car for his personal use. The campaign train, with Presidential candidates making speeches from the rear platforms on the observation cars, has become a political tradition in this country. Yet we may have seen the last of these. President Eisenhower seldom rode in his luxurious private car, the *Ferdinand Magellan*; he preferred to travel by automobile or airplane. In January, 1959, the car was retired from service and turned over to the University of Miami to be placed on exhibit on the campus.

The *Ferdinand Magellan* was built for President Franklin D. Roosevelt in World War II. It is armor-plated, with bullet-proof windows three inches thick, and weighs almost twice as much as an ordinary Pullman car.

President Roosevelt liked to roll along at a moderate thirty-five miles an hour, but President Harry S. Truman was always in a hurry. He would tell the engineer to open the throttle and hit seventy-five miles per hour or more.

Back in the days when dollars would buy much more than they will today, wealthy people sometimes hired whole trains for special excursions. In 1870, the Boston Board of Trade chartered a train of Pullman cars to make the first trip by rail from the Atlantic Coast to the Pacific Coast. A daily newspaper, the *Trans-Continental*, was published in the baggage car.

Six weeks after they set out, the party returned to Boston. They had seen the mighty Mississippi River, the Great Plains, the Rocky Mountains, the Mormon colony at Salt Lake City, the Sierra Nevadas, and glamorous San Francisco. Everyone agreed it had been a marvelous trip. "Hurrah for the railroad!" exclaimed Editor W. R. Steele in an issue of the *Trans-Continental*.

In 1905, a very wealthy and eccentric Californian, Walter Scott, better known as "Death Valley Scotty," asked the Santa Fe Railroad to provide a special train to take him to Chicago in a hurry. The next day the train pulled out of Los Angeles and raced to Chicago, with its lone passenger, in 44 hours and 54 minutes. This was a full thirteen hours less than the previous record for the trip. "Death Valley Scotty" paid $5,500 for his fast ride.

The New York Central's famous Empire State Express, with engine No. 999 at full throttle, reached a speed of 112.5 miles an hour on May 10, 1893. No human had ever traveled this fast before. The Broadway Limited of the Pennsylvania Railroad is considered by most rail historians to hold the all-time United States rail speed record of 127.06 mph, set on June 12, 1905, in Ohio.

The Union Pacific's diesel train, City of Portland, made a coast-to-coast run from Los Angeles to New York City in October, 1934, in 56 hours and 55 minutes, including all stops on its 3,258-mile journey. This

Uniformed Harvey Girls pose in front of a Harvey hotel in Wallace, Kansas.

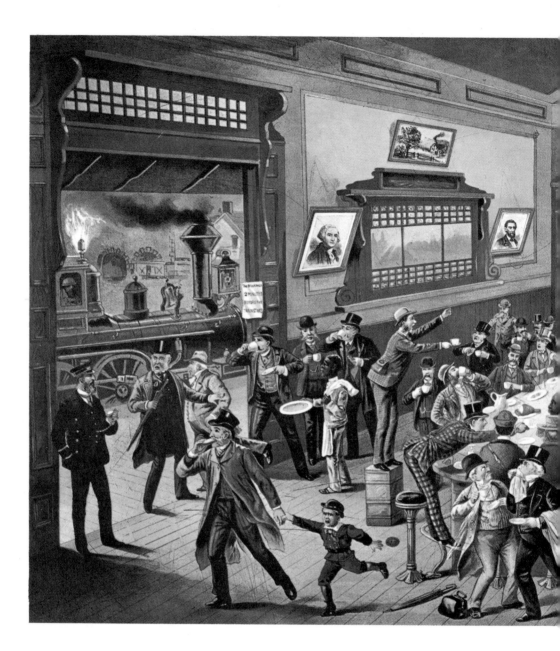

is an average of almost a mile a minute. The record still stands, and it seems doubtful that any effort ever will be made to break it.

While railroads long ago gave up the sentimental practice of giving a name to their locomotives, they still advertise a number of passenger trains by name. Perhaps the best known trains in America have been the New York Central's 20th Century Limited from New York to Chicago, and the Santa Fe's Super Chief from Chicago to Los Angeles. For many years these trains carried movie stars and financiers on their transcontinental journeys.

Two passenger trains are named

Before dining cars were added to trains, the station lunch room was a busy place during the ten-minute refreshment stop.

Cincinnati. Pocahontas was an Indian maiden, who, according to a famous legend, was said to have saved Captain John Smith's life after her father ordered him killed.

The Lackawanna Railroad runs the Phoebe Snow, a luxurious passenger train named after a girl who never existed except in the imagination of the company's advertising department.

Sixty years ago the Lackawanna was one of the few United States railroads burning hard anthracite coal in locomotive fireboxes. This type of coal did not produce so much soot and cinders to soil the clothing of passengers. So the Lackawanna's advertising would feature a sketch of Phoebe Snow, a pretty girl in a white dress, offering this testimonial:

I won my fame and wide acclaim
    For Lackawanna's splendid name
By keeping bright and snowy white
    Upon the Road of Anthracite.

Nowadays this train speeds along daily between New York and Buffalo, pulled by a diesel locomotive that puts out no cinders at all. And the Lackawanna's freight cars travel all over the United States and Canada proclaiming their loyalty to "The Route of Phoebe Snow."

for famous women in American history. The Ann Rutledge honors the memory of a girl who was once believed to have been Abraham Lincoln's sweetheart. It runs between Chicago and St. Louis on the Gulf, Mobile and Ohio Railroad.

The Norfolk & Western operates the Pocahontas between Norfolk and

127

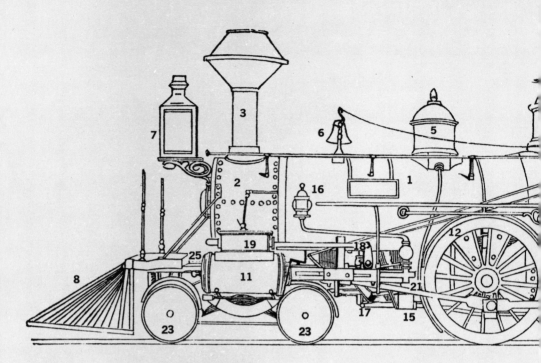

1. Boiler
2. Smoke Box
3. Diamond Smokestack,
   or Chimney
4. Safety Valve

5. Sand Box
6. Bell
7. Headlamp
8. Cowcatcher
9. Whistle

10. Cab
11. Cylinder
12. Leading Driving Wheel
    (connected to the steam cylinder)
13. Trailing Driving Wheel

AN AMERICAN LOCOMOTIVE, 1872

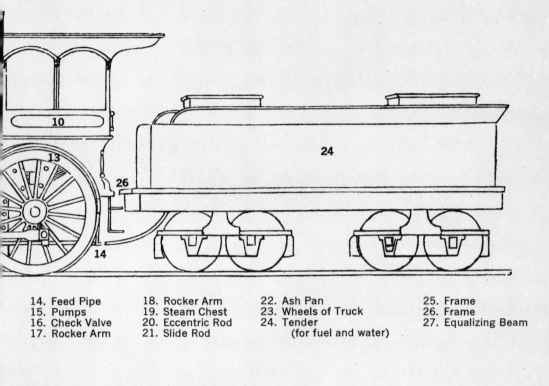

14. Feed Pipe	18. Rocker Arm	22. Ash Pan	25. Frame
15. Pumps	19. Steam Chest	23. Wheels of Truck	26. Frame
16. Check Valve	20. Eccentric Rod	24. Tender	27. Equalizing Beam
17. Rocker Arm	21. Slide Rod	(for fuel and water)	

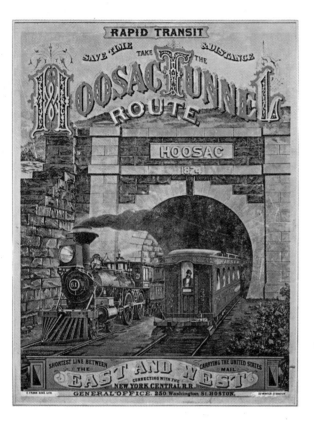

MARVELS OF
ENGINEERING SKILL

Because smooth-wheeled locomotives cannot pull heavy cars up steep hills, railroad engineers were forced to build high bridges and dig long tunnels to smooth the path for trains.

American railroads now use about 1,400 tunnels, ranging in length from the thirty-foot Bee Rock Tunnel on the Louisville & Nashville Railroad, to the Great Northern Railway's Cascade Tunnel, through which trains run underground for nearly eight miles.

Three railroads, the Southern Pacific, the Missouri Pacific and the Texas & Pacific, share the longest railroad-highway bridge in the nation—the 4.4-mile Huey Long Bridge across the Mississippi River above New Orleans. The 192,000 railroad bridges now in use in the United States, could they be joined together, would stretch 4,500 miles—the distance from New York to Naples, Italy.

By means of their skill, America's railway engineers bridged, graded, and tunneled their way across the nation, until every corner of it was caught up in a web of shining rails.

A poster for the Fitchburg Railroad (above) advertises the 4.73-mile Hoosac Tunnel, which was cut through the Berkshire Mountains of Massachusetts in 1876, after having taken 21 years to build. The photograph (below) shows a narrow-gauge train threading its way through Lost Souls Canyon, between Silverton and Durango, Colorado, in 1885.

In 1876, engineers of the Southern Pacific completed the Tehachapi Loop in the Tehachapi Mountains between San Francisco and Los Angeles. Its curving track permitted the road-bed to be raised 2734 feet within a space of sixteen miles as the crow flies. A modern engineering wonder—the freight yard at Houston, Texas (below)—makes the shunting of freight cars almost entirely automatic, by means of radar and an "electronic brain."

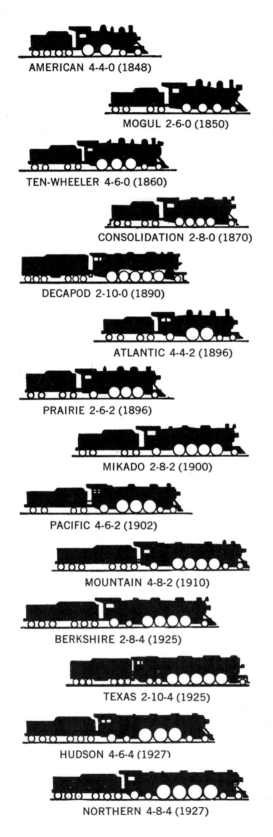

AMERICAN 4-4-0 (1848)

MOGUL 2-6-0 (1850)

TEN-WHEELER 4-6-0 (1860)

CONSOLIDATION 2-8-0 (1870)

DECAPOD 2-10-0 (1890)

ATLANTIC 4-4-2 (1896)

PRAIRIE 2-6-2 (1896)

MIKADO 2-8-2 (1900)

PACIFIC 4-6-2 (1902)

MOUNTAIN 4-8-2 (1910)

BERKSHIRE 2-8-4 (1925)

TEXAS 2-10-4 (1925)

HUDSON 4-6-4 (1927)

NORTHERN 4-8-4 (1927)

TYPES OF STEAM

The first successful locomotives, built in Great Britain, carried all their weight on their four drive wheels. This gave them great pulling power, but Americans found these engines too heavy for the light rails used in this country.

A machinist for the Mohawk and Hudson railroad, John B. Jervis, decided to add more wheels and lighten the load each wheel would transmit to the tracks. By replacing two of the drive wheels with a swiveling four-wheel truck, his engine—the forerunner of the American type—rounded curves more easily. and did less damage to the rails.

Other designs followed. Engines with large boilers and a few large drivers proved best for high speed passenger service. More and smaller drive wheels, which carried a larger proportion of the engine's weight, provided the greater power and traction needed for heavy-duty freight service.

Soon there were so many kinds of locomotives in use that a system was needed for distinguishing one type of engine from another. The Whyte System, named after Frederic M. Whyte, general mechanical engineer for the New York Central, came into use in 1900, to help simplify matters. In the Whyte System, an engine's wheels are numbered (for example, 4-4-0) as in the column at left. The first digit refers

TWO-TRUCK SHAY (1883)

SWITCHER 0-6-0 (1902)

LOCOMOTIVES

to the number of small wheels in the pilot truck at the front of the locomotive. The next number tells how many drive wheels are linked to the steam cylinders. Last comes the number of wheels, if any, in the trailing truck under the cab.

The dates in parenthesis, at left, refer to the approximate year in which the named locomotives came into use. The classic American 4-4-0—which followed "teakettle" engines of the Tom Thumb type—was the first practical locomotive to be widely used. Other woodburning types came shortly thereafter, such as the Moguls, Ten-Wheelers, and Consolidations. After 1870, most locomotives were powered by coal.

The Consolidation was the most popular type of all time: 33,000 of them were built over the years. Larger and larger freight engines, such as the Decapod, Prairie, Mikado, Berkshire, and Texas were built from 1890 to 1925. Famous passenger types, such as the Atlantic, Pacific, and Hudson came into being. Engines especially designed for climbing mountain grades were also perfected. At last, designers turned out enormous mountain-climbing locomotives such as the Articulated and the Challenger, with so many drive wheels that it was necessary to hinge the bodies of their engines in the middle, so that they could go around curves.

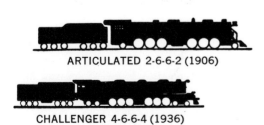

ARTICULATED 2-6-6-2 (1906)

CHALLENGER 4-6-6-4 (1936)

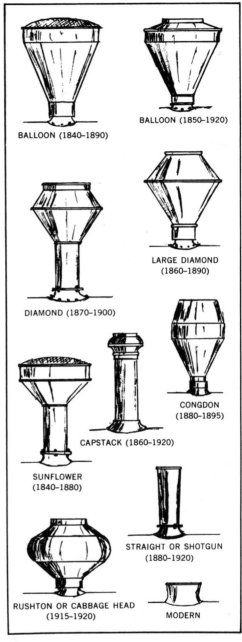

BALLOON (1840–1890)

BALLOON (1850–1920)

LARGE DIAMOND (1860–1890)

DIAMOND (1870–1900)

CONGDON (1880–1895)

CAPSTACK (1860–1920)

SUNFLOWER (1840–1880)

STRAIGHT OR SHOTGUN (1880–1920)

RUSHTON OR CABBAGE HEAD (1915–1920)

MODERN

TYPES OF SMOKESTACKS

There was always danger that flying sparks from the smokestacks of wood-burning or coal-burning locomotives would set fire to the surrounding forest or prairie. To prevent this, designers used various kinds of cinder traps and screened "bonnets" on stacks, to catch and hold the hot clinkers. The Large Diamond, Sunflower, Cabbage Head and Balloons were used on wood-burners. The Diamond, Shotgun, Capstack and Congdon were used chiefly on coal-burning engines.

LEGEND AND ROMANCE

Kate Shelley, the 15-year-old daughter of a Chicago and North Western Railway section hand, looked through the window of the family farmhouse one stormy night in 1881 as a locomotive pushed slowly out onto a trestle spanning a swollen creek. This was a pilot locomotive, Kate knew, sent ahead to test the safety of bridges and trestles for the fast Atlantic Express train which would be coming along soon.

A cloudburst had hit the state of Iowa, and her father along with all the other C & NW trackworkers were hard at work repairing washouts and rebuilding bridges.

As Kate watched in horror, the trestle across Honey Creek began to sag under the weight of the engine. Then it swayed and collapsed, plunging the locomotive and four crewmen into the torrent. Two men were swept away, but Kate saw the others clinging desperately to treetops as the flood waters raced past.

Kate Shelley knew what she must do. The engineer of the Atlantic Express must be warned before his train with its hundreds of innocent passengers came thundering along to hit the broken trestle and plunge to destruction, too. The nearest sta-

tion where the Express could be flagged down was Moingona, on the other side of the raging Des Moines

The railroad linked the quiet, small towns of America to the promise of the big city.

River. To get there, Kate would have to walk across the ties of a 550-foot railroad bridge in the storm.

But Kate Shelley was a brave girl, and a loyal railroadman's daughter. She lit her lantern and started out.

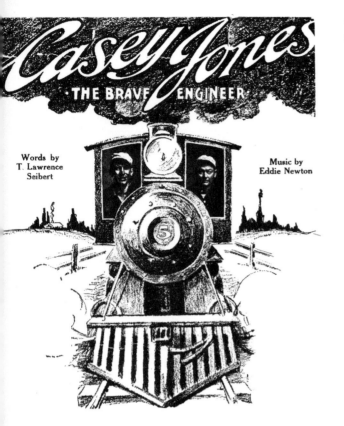

Words by
T. Lawrence
Seibert

Music by
Eddie Newton

The brave engineer, Casey Jones, became
the hero of a musical comedy in 1901.

for this brave deed. There is a Kate Shelley lodge of the Brotherhood of Railway Trainmen. A Kate Shelley memorial fountain stands in Dubuque, Iowa. In 1956, on the 75th anniversary of that black night when the Atlantic Express was saved, the Order of Railway Conductors and Brakemen placed beside Kate Shelley's grave a memorial plaque bearing these words:

"Hers is a deed bound for legend —a story to be told until the last order fades and the last rail rusts."

Some of the railroad legends do not have such happy endings. For example, there is the tragic and true story of Casey Jones.

Casey's real name was John

Halfway across the bridge the gale blew out the light. Now she had only fitful flashes of lightning to guide her steps across the trembling bridge. One misstep, and she would tumble to her death in the raging waters below. Kate kept going.

She reached Moingona and told the station agent what had happened. He flagged down the Atlantic Express, and a rescue locomotive was sent back across the bridge to haul the surviving crewmen of the pilot engine to safety.

Kate Shelley is remembered and honored by railroadmen everywhere

Reading's No. 44, seen with her crew.

Luther Jones. Because he came from Cayce, Kentucky, his fellow workers gave him the nickname of "Casey."

In February, 1900, Casey was assigned to the fastest train on the Illinois Central Railroad, the Cannonball Express, carrying the mail between Chicago and New Orleans. Casey had the difficult run between Memphis, Tennessee, and Canton, Mississippi; 188 miles of sharp curves and steep grades.

On April 30, 1900, Casey and his faithful Negro fireman, Sim Webb, pulled out of Memphis at fifty minutes after midnight with a train of twelve coaches. The Cannonball Express had lost an hour and fifteen minutes running south from Chicago, and Casey was determined to make up the time. He almost succeeded. At some places along his run, the big ten-wheeler locomotive, No. 382, must have been racing along at more than a hundred miles an hour, for the train was only two minutes behind schedule when disaster struck at Vaughan, Mississippi, twelve miles from Canton.

A freight train was taking the siding at Vaughan to clear the track for the Cannonball Express when an air hose broke on one of the boxcars. The brakes locked, stalling the freight train with the caboose and several cars still on the main line. The train crew worked frantically to repair the hose and release the brakes, but there was not time. Down the track they could see the

Casey Jones

Kate Shelley

glow of Casey's headlight through the fog and darkness, and hear the rackety exhaust of the speeding locomotive

In the cab, Casey looked ahead and spotted the faint gleam of the red bull's-eye lanterns on the caboose ahead.

"Jump, Sim!" he shouted to the fireman. "Unload!" In the same instant he "dynamited" his engine, yanking the Johnson bar into reverse, setting the air brakes and opening wide the chutes from the steam dome to give his spinning drivers a grip on the rails.

Its whistle shrieking a warning, No. 382 ploughed into the caboose, shattering it to kindling wood. The next car, full of baled hay, and the next, loaded with shelled corn, were split open and their contents sent flying. Casey's engine leaped off the rails and swerved around with its smashed front end pointing back toward the north.

Inside the cab, Casey Jones lay dead, an iron bolt driven through his neck and a broken bale of hay covering his body. Sim Webb jumped just before the collision, and landed in some bushes. The express messenger, A. J. Stein, was thrown heavily to the floor of the express car. These two men spent a long time in a hospital recovering from their injuries, but no one else was hurt, thanks to Casey Jones.

Like Kate Shelley, the name of Casey Jones will be remembered "till the last rail rusts." A Negro roundhouse worker, Wallace Saunders, wrote a famous ballad about Casey's last run, which begins:

"Come all you rounders if you
want to hear
The story told about a brave
engineer. . ."

A railroad engineer nowadays may operate a different locomotive each time he makes a run. But in the old days a railroad would assign a locomotive to each engineer, and he would take it on each trip unless it was in the roundhouse for repairs. Engineers took great pride in their locomotives, and after each run they would see to it that every smudge of soot or grease was cleaned from the boiler and drivers. Brass or nickel parts were kept polished, and paint work never was allowed to become scratched or faded.

When an engineer received a new locomotive, often he would take with him the whistle and headlight from the old one. Early day locomotive

The Highland Light (1867) *had a sunflower stack and was decorated lavishly. It was one of the last of the splendid, ornate engines that once ruled the rails.*

139

builders delivered them without headlights because so many engineers preferred to install their own big storm lanterns, often handsomely decorated with colorful landscapes enameled on their sides by artistic friends.

The first steam locomotives were crude and ugly, but as the years passed their designers gave a great deal of thought to their appearance. William Mason, a locomotive builder in Taunton, Massachusetts, once declared they ought to "look

The disastrous wreck of the Old 97, made immortal in a ballad, took place in 1903 in Virginia; thirteen people died.

bilt of the New York Central put an end to the era of fancy trimmings on steam engines. When the public began criticizing the wealth and power of the railroads, after the Civil War, word went around that the Commodore's private locomotive was plated with gold. Much annoyed, the Commodore ordered all the brass and bright enamel on NYC locomotives completely covered with black paint.

Many famous writers have been enchanted by steam engines. Here is how Henry David Thoreau once described a speeding locomotive: ". . . I hear the iron horse make the hills echo with his snort like thunder, shaking the earth with his feet, and breathing fire and smoke from his nostrils . . . ."

So that Thoreau's thunder of the locomotive may not be completely forgotten, many railroads offered some of their steam engines to museums and city parks (see list on page 150) to be placed on exhibit as a reminder of the old days of railroading. In years to come, children who have not had the thrill of riding in a train pulled by a steam locomotive at least will be able to see and climb over an old iron horse, even though its boiler is cold and its whistle forever silent.

somewhat better than cookstoves on wheels." One of his engines, the *Highland Light*, built in 1867 for the Cape Cod Central Railroad, is regarded as the most handsome steam locomotive in railroad history.

Crusty old Commodore Vander-

FAREWELL TO STEAM

America and the iron horse grew up together. In the 1830's and 1840's, railroads linked together the cities of the Atlantic seaboard, and began poking their way through the Appalachians. By 1852, more than nine thousand miles of rails had been built, and trains delivered freight and passengers as far west across the prairies as Chicago.

Only seventeen years later, in 1869, locomotives were able to sweep across the broad Nebraska plains, over the Rockies, over the deserts of Utah, to climb the Sierra Nevadas, and to end their run in the Central Pacific depot in Sacramento. By 1880, there were 94,000 miles of rails binding the Union together; by 1900, 193,000 miles.

As the railroads grew, the country grew. Before the Civil War, America was an agricultural nation, a land where most of the people lived on farms. After the Civil War, when more railroads were built than ever

To generations of Americans, the very meaning of speed and power was to be found in the huge driving wheels of such locomotives as this giant 4-8-4.

before, America became a manufacturing nation, where most of the people lived in towns and cities.

This big change could never have come about without the railroads. America was a big country and needed fast, cheap, easy transportation. Railroads brought coal and oil, iron ore and cotton to the factories. They hauled away steel, machines, cloth, and other finished products. They carried beef, sheep, and wheat from farms in the West to cities in the East. And they carried people everywhere. Most of the emigrants who settled Minnesota, the Dakotas, Nebraska, and Kansas in the 1870's and 1880's traveled west by train.

No town could grow without the railroad. Towns that became rail junctions grew into large cities. Towns that were bypassed by the railroad remained small or faded away altogether. At the end of World War I, more than 254,000 miles of track and 65,000 steam locomotives gave America the greatest rail system in the world.

Even the smallest of towns had a link to the outside world—if it was on a railroad line. The arrival of the train was always a big event. Anxious passengers on the depot platform checked their watches to see if the "Limited" was going to be on time. Crates, baggage, ice, and mail were wheeled out for loading. Then, even before the train was heard or seen, the rails began to hum and the earth began to tremble.

When at last the engine appeared it seemed to grow huge in an instant. Its bell clanged wildly over the hoarse "chuff, chuff," of the engine. Jets of white steam hissed about the drive wheels as a huge black column of smoke boiled up from the towering smokestack.

As soon as the demon had swallowed freight and passengers, it was ready to take up its journey again. The conductor closed the case of his watch, and the brakeman raised and lowered his kerosene lantern. The bell rang. The twenty-ton locomotive shuddered, gathered speed and with a clacking of rails, began thundering away. The brightly lighted windows of Pullmans and diners flashed by, as the train carried its fortunate passengers off into the great world.

The red lights on the last car grew smaller and smaller until they disappeared around the bend. The ghostly wail of the whistle echoed back from the hills. At last the train was gone.

To the little crowd on the station platform the train meant speed, power, progress, and adventure. Passenger engines averaged forty to sixty miles per hour. And they could do better on special runs.

Commuting by train—which had become common by 1895 when this photograph was taken in Chicago's Randolph Street station—increased the growth of suburbs.

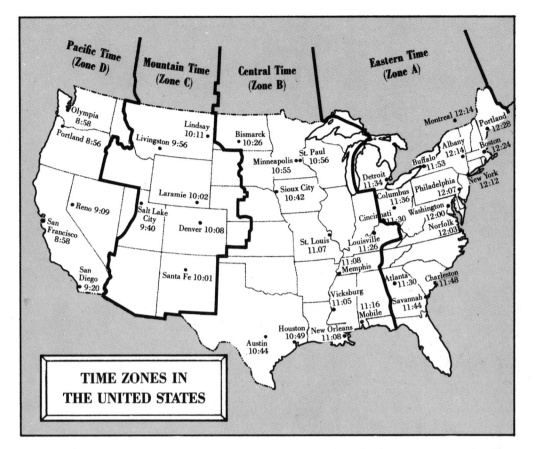

Pacific Time
(Zone D)
Mountain Time
(Zone C)
Central Time
(Zone B)
Eastern Time
(Zone A)

Olympia 8:58
Portland 8:56
Lindsay 10:11
Livingston 9:56
Bismarck 10:26
Montreal 12:14
Portland 12:28
Albany 12:14
Boston 12:24
Minneapolis 10:55
St. Paul 10:56
Buffalo 11:53
New York 12:12
Laramie 10:02
Sioux City 10:42
Detroit 11:34
Columbus 11:36
Philadelphia 12:07
Reno 9:09
San Francisco 8:58
Salt Lake City 9:40
Denver 10:08
Cincinnati 11:30
Washington 12:00
Norfolk 12:03
St. Louis 11.07
Louisville 11:26
San Diego 9:20
Santa Fe 10:01
11:08 Memphis
Atlanta 11:30
Charleston 11:48
Vicksburg 11:05
Savannah 11:44
11:16 Mobile
Houston 10:49
New Orleans 11:08
Austin 10:44

TIME ZONES IN
THE UNITED STATES

*The railroads gave the United States its present Standard Time zones. As the
railroads added more trains, they had to be able to schedule them accurately to
avoid accidents; this was impossible, as long as each city set its own time. In
1870 Charles F. Dowd, a school teacher, organized the original four-zone system.
After November 18, 1883, when the railroads persuaded Congress to adopt Dowd's
plan, all of the cities in Zone A agreed to operate on the same time. In other
words, the cities of Albany, Norfolk and Charleston, for example, reached 12:00
noon at the same instant. At the same moment all the cities in Zone B reached
11:00 A.M.; all those in Zone C reached 10:00 A.M.; and all those in Zone D
reached 9:00 A.M. Before Dowd's plan went into effect—when cities operated on
"sun time"—trainmen running between New York City and Buffalo, for example,
had had to account for a nineteen-minute difference in time. The difference was
caused by the fact that clocks in each city had been set at 12:00 noon as soon
as the sun reached its highest point in the sky. This was confusing, as the
sun stood overhead at different times—depending upon the location of the city.*

Trains could go anywhere, over
rivers and prairies, over deserts and
mountains. They brought cities
closer together. In 1812, it took six
days to go from Pittsburgh to Philadelphia by stagecoach. In 1854, the
same journey took fifteen hours by
rail. By 1920 the time was down to
five hours.

The coming of the railroad ended
an age of slow-moving transportation. Even though enormous loads of
freight still move by tugboat and
barge on the rivers of America, the

railroad drove many canal companies out of business. It ended passenger service on riverboats and on stagecoach lines. It did away with the enormous oxen-trains of wagons which used to carry freight across the Plains.

For years the railroads reigned supreme, carrying the bulk of all freight to the cities; and swelling their populations. For railroads,

more than any other factor, helped the spread of suburbs.

Until the end of World War I, no form of transportation came close to challenging the railroad. But after 1918, with the building of good roads, trucks began carrying huge amounts of freight. More and more people began to travel by car, bus, and plane. In the 1950's, many railroads cut down passenger service,

This small, wood-burning engine, which was built in 1891, ran until recently on a logging railroad line in South Carolina.

and closed some branch lines entirely. The total mileage of rail lines has shrunk from 254,000 miles in 1918, to 219,000 miles in 1959. Railroads have now lost so much business—they are carrying only four per cent of the nation's passenger traffic today—that many people believe that they will have to receive help from goverment in order to survive.

At the same time, railroads are carrying forty-five per cent of the freight traffic. They are still doing a tremendously important job—a job which no other form of transportation can do as well. It seems unlikely that they will ever wholly disappear.

Of course, the railroad of today is not the same as the railroad of yesterday. In 1924 the oil-burning diesel engine was introduced. Cleaner, more powerful, and cheaper to operate, it has almost entirely replaced the coal-burning steam locomotive.

Of the 65,000 steam locomotives in use in 1924, there are now only 325 in active service—so few that city parks and museums have begun to set up exhibits where the iron horse can be seen.

But to Americans of not so long ago the locomotive was more than a machine. It meant freedom and power. And the railroad was more than just a means of transportation. It was the fastest way to get from the farm to the Big City, from Nowhere to Someplace. The steam locomotive is part of American history, and Americans will never forget it. Nor will they forget the engine's long sweet whistle, sounding in the night, with its call to adventure and its promise of success.

A GLOSSARY OF RAILROADING SLANG

Although few of today's railroad men make use of the words in this list, many were part of the everyday speech of the yard hands, engineers, and conductors of an earlier generation.

AIR MONKEY—Air-brake repairman

BABY-LIFTER—Passenger brakeman

BAD ORDER—Car in need of repair

BAKEHEAD—Locomotive fireman; also bell-ringer, blackie, etc.

BALLAST SCORCHER—Speedy engineer

BALL OF FIRE—Fast run

BARN—Engine house

BEANERY—Railroad eating-house

BEANERY QUEEN—A waitress

BINDLE STIFF or BLANKET STIFF—Hobo who totes a blanket and uses it wherever night finds him. (Bindle is a corruption of "bundle")

BOOMER—Railroadman who changes jobs frequently

CABOOSE—Chariot, Buggy, Parlor, Hack, Palace, Hay-wagon, Doghouse, Crummy, Crumb Box, Crib, etc.

CAPTAIN—Conductor

CASEY JONES—Any locomotive engineer, especially a fast one

CINDER DICK—Railroad detective

CINDER SNAPPER—Railroad enthusiast who rides open platform on observation car

COAL HEAVER—Fireman, or stoker

CONSIST—Make up of the train (cars)

CORNFIELD MEET—A head-on collision

DEADHEAD—A person riding on a pass

DOUSE THE GLIM—Extinguish a lantern

DRONE CAGE—Private car

FLIMSY—Train order

GANDY DANCER—Track laborer, so called from the gander-like motions of a man tamping ties; another version is that this term is derived from the name of an old Irish jig

GATE—A switch

GREEN EYE—Clear signal

HEAD END—Front end of train

HIGHBALL—A "clear track" signal

HIGH IRON—Main track line

HOG—A locomotive

HOGGER or HOGHEAD—Engineer

HOLE—A sidetrack for passing trains

HOTSHOT—Fast train

JAM BUSTER—Assistant yardmaster

JOHNSON BAR—Reverse lever on a locomotive

LIZARD SCORCHER—Dining-car chef

Scenes like this one—in Raton Pass, Texas, in 1951—become more and more rare as railroads continue to replace steam locomotives with more efficient Diesels.

MASTER MANIAC—Master mechanic

PRIVATE VARNISH—Private passenger car

RAP THE SACK—Give the locomotive a wide-open throttle for more speed.

RATTLER—Freight train

RED BALL—Fast freight

RIP TRACK—Where cars are repaired

SHACK—A brakeman

SIDEWINDER—Shay geared locomotive

SLIM GAUGE—Trains and tracks of less than the conventional 4′ 8½″ width

SPOTTER—Company spy

STAR GAZER—Brakeman who fails to see signals

STRAWBERRY PATCH—Rear end of caboose by night; also railroad yard studded with red lights

STRAW BOSS—Foreman of small gang or acting foreman

TANGENT—Straight track

VARNISH—Passenger cars

WIDEN ON HER—Open the throttle, increase speed

WING HER—Set brakes on moving train

ZULUS—Immigrants traveling by rail

Rock of Ages, *once operated by a quarrying line in Barre, Vermont, is now retired.*

APPENDIX

AMERICAN HERITAGE PUBLISHING CO., INC. · BOOK DIVISION: Richard M. Ketchum, *Editor*. JUNIOR LIBRARY: Ferdinand N. Monjo, *Editor*, John Ratti, *Assistant Editor*. Malabar Schleiter · Judy Sheftel · Julia B. Potts · Mary Leverty, *Editorial Assistants. Designed by Jos. Trautwein.*

STEAM LOCOMOTIVES ON DISPLAY   There are far too many museums throughout the United States where steam locomotives are on display, for them to be listed in their entirety; readers desiring complete information may write The Association of American Railroads, Transportation Building, Washington 6, D. C., for their booklet, *Steam Locomotives on Display in the United States.* A few of the largest collections are listed below; an asterisk denotes locations where steam engines can be seen not only on display, but in action as well.
* Travel Town, Griffith Park, Los Angeles, California
    Operates a narrow-gauge railroad through the seven-acre portion of Griffith Park
  Baltimore and Ohio Transportation Museum, Baltimore, Maryland
* Edaville RR and Museum (F. Nelson Blount Collection) South Carver, Massachusetts
* Pleasure Island (F. Nelson Blount Collection) Wakefield, Massachusetts
  Henry Ford Museum & Greenfield Village, Dearborn, Michigan
* National Museum of Transport, St. Louis, Missouri

ACKNOWLEDGMENTS   The editors are deeply grateful to Mr. Lawrence W. Sagle of the Baltimore and Ohio Transportation Museum for his unfailing assistance; to Dr. Edgar Breitenbach, Curator of Prints at the Library of Congress for his cooperation in furnishing old posters and lithographs heretofore unpublished; and to Mrs. Bella Landauer of the New York Historical Society for generously making available her personal collection. In addition they wish expressly to thank the following individuals and organizations for their kindness in providing pictorial materials from their collections: Association of American Railroads—Mr. George Martin; Free Library of Philadelphia—Miss Dorothy Hale Litchfield; Museum of the City of New York—Mr. Albert Baragwanath; New York Central—Mr. David Beadle; Kansas State Historical Society—Mr. Robert Richmond; George Eastman House, Rochester—Mr. Beaumont Newhall; and Mr. Arnold Eagle, Photographer.

PICTURE CREDITS

The source of each picture used in this book is listed below, by page. When two or more pictures appear on one page, they are separated by semi-colons. The following abbreviations are used:
BLC—Bella Landauer Collection, New York Historical Society
NYHS—New York Historical Society
MCNY—Museum of the City of New York, the Harry T. Peters Collection

UPRR—Union Pacific Railroad
NYPL—New York Public Library
LC—Library of Congress
C&I—Currier and Ives
CC—Coverdale and Colpitts
SPRR—Southern Pacific Railroad
MHS—Maryland Historical Society
KSHS—Kansas State Historical Society
WCBA—Warshaw Collection of Business Americana

Cover—C&I—MCNY. **Front endsheet** (left to right, top) LC; WCBA; KSHS; (bot.) Culver Service; LC. 5 Southern Railway. 6–7 "On the Road" by Thomas Otter—Nelson Gallery, Atkins Museum, Kansas City, Mo. 9 Hulton Picture Library, London. 10 "Country Road with Oxcart" by Benjamin H. Latrobe—MHS. 11 (top) Transportation Library, University of Michigan; (bot.) "Lockport on Erie Canal" by Mary Keys—Munson-Williams-Proctor Institute. 12 Science Museum, London. 13 (top) Delaware and Hudson RR; (bot.) Science Museum, London. 14 (top) Kennedy Galleries; (bot.) Science Museum, London. 15 "Locomotion No. 1," drawing by J. R. Browne—Science Museum, London. 16 Alexander Robb—Museum of Science and Industry, Chicago. 17 (top, both) Pullman Co.; (bot.) Smithsonian Institution. 18 (top) AAR; (center) BLC; (bot.) Peale Museum, Baltimore. 19 (center and bot.) Peale Museum, Baltimore. 20 (both) AAR. 21 (top) Southern RR; (bot.) Stevens Institute. 22–23 (all) CC. 24 MHS. 25 BLC. 26 National Archives. 27 Carnegie Institution of Washington. 28–29 Free Library of Philadelphia. 30 AAR. 31 Culver Service. 32–33 "Panorama of Andrews Raid" by Thomas C. Gordon—Henry Ford Museum. 34 LC. 35 LC. 36 "Sherman's March to the Sea" engraving by Ritchie—Old Print Shop. 37 Matthew Brady—LC. 38–39 "Driving of the Last Spike" by Thomas Hill—State of California, Dept. of Finance, Sacramento, California. 40 UPRR. 41 UPRR. 42–43 "Destruction of Railroad Track by Cheyenne Indians" by Jacob Gogolin—KSHS. 44 UPRR. 45 UPRR. 46–47 "Snow Sheds on the Central Pacific Railroad in the Sierra Nevada Mountains" by Joseph Becker—Eliot Elisofon, Courtesy LIFE Magazine. 48 SPRR. 50 C&I—MCNY. 51 UPRR. 52 (both) UPRR. 53 SPRR. 54–55 C&I—MCNY. 56 (left to right) Culver Service NYPL; Culver Service. 57 (top) Brown Bros. (bot.) Culver Service. 58–59 CC. 60 NYHS. 61 Culver Service. 62–63 CC. 64 (left to right) Brown Bros.; SPRR; Brown Bros.; SPRR. 64–65 Map drawn expressly for this book by Elmer Smith (left) Brown Bros.; (right) Culver Service. 65 (both) Culver Service. 66–67 Judge, 1885—NYHS. 68 (top) Brown Bros.; (center) Great Northern RR; (bot.) Culver Service. 70–71 "Sacramento Station" by William Hahn—M. H. de Young Museum, San Francisco. 73 "Held up" by N. H. Trotter—Smithsonian Institution. 74 LC. 75 KSHS.

76 WCBA. 77 "Cheyenne Indians Attack Workers" by J. Gogolin—KSHS. 78 Culver Service. 80 NYPL. 81 *Mountains and Molehills* by Frank Marryat—NYHS. 82 (top) Harper's Weekly, 1874—NYPL; (bot.) Philip Ashton Rollins Collection, Princeton Library. 83 Leslie's Weekly, 1871—LC. 84–85 LC. 86 LC. 87 UPRR. 88–89 C&I—MCNY. 90 LC. 90–91 Map drawn expressly for this book by Elmer Smith; (bot.) UPRR. 92 (top) BLC: (bot.) "Outward the Quay of Dublin" by T. H. Maguire—NYHS 93 LC. 94 Lewis Hine—George Eastman House, Rochester, New York. 95 (top) Culver Service; (bot.) Nebraska State Historical Society, Lincoln, Nebr. 96 "Accident on the Western Maryland Railroad" by Frederick Dielman—MHS. 98–99 "The Catastrophe at Meudon" by Plattel—Collection Lichtenberg, Courtesy Dolfuss, Paris. 101 New York Central. 102–103 C&I—LC. 104 (both) AAR. 105 (top) Bettmann Archive; (bot.) AAR. 106–107 C&I—LC. 108 Collection Mrs. Zelda P. Mackay, San Francisco. 109 Culver Service. 110 C&I—LC. 111 BLC. 112 Leslie's Illustrated Weekly, 1877—NYHS. 114–115 Free Library of Philadelphia. 116 Brown Bros. 117 (top) Lucius Beebe; (bot.) Harper's Weekly, 1894. 118 C&I—LC. 119 C&I—LC. 120 (top) Illinois Central RR; (bot.) Harper's Weekly, 1858. 121 Transportation Museum, University of Michigan. 122 BLC. 123 (both) LC. 124 Lucius Beebe. 125 Santa Fe RR. 126–127 Chicago Historical Society. 128–129 Culver Service. 130 (top) CC; (bot.) Denver Public Library Western Collection. 131 (both) SPRR. 132–133 Practical Guide to Model Railroading; smokestack sketches by David Beadle, New York Central. 134–135 "Manchester Valley" by Joseph Pickett—Collection, Museum of Modern Art, New York, Gift of Mrs. John D. Rockefeller, Jr. 136 (top) BLC; (bot.) Reading Co., Philadelphia. 137 (top) Illinois Central System; (bot.) Order of RR Conductors and Brakemen. 138–139 "Ghosts of Engines" by Lux Feininger—Museum of Modern Art, New York, Gift of the Griffis Foundation; (bot.) CC. 140–141 Southern RR. 142–143 Trains Magazine. 144 Map drawn expressly for this book by Elmer Smith. 145 Trains Magazine. 146–147 Picture by Oliver O. Jensen. 148–149 Trains Magazine; Rail Photo Service: Geo. C. Corey. 150 Picture by Oliver O. Jensen. **Back endsheet**—(left to right) LC; CC; BLC: (bot.) WCBA; CC. **Back Cover**—(left to right, top) Smithsonian Institution; C&I—MCNY; (center) Old Print Shop; (bot.) CC; CC.

BIBLIOGRAPHY

Adams, Charles Francis, Jr. *A Chapter of Erie*. Boston: Fields Osgood & Company, 1869.

Alexander, E. P. *Iron Horses: American Locomotives, 1829–1900*. New York: W. W. Norton & Company, Inc., 1941.

American Railroads; Their Growth and Development. Washington, D. C.: Association of American Railroads, 1958.

Athearn, Robert G. *William Tecumseh Sherman and the Settlement of the West*. Norman: University of Oklahoma Press, 1956.

Beebe, Lucius, and Clegg, Charles. *The Age of Steam*. New York: Rinehart & Company, Inc., 1957.

Beebe. *Hear the Train Blow*. New York: E. P. Dutton & Co., 1952.

Beebe. *Narrow Gauge in the Rockies*. Berkeley, California: The Howell-North Press, 1958.

Block, Eugene B. *Great Train Robberies of the West*. New York: Coward-McCann, Inc., 1959.

Clark, William H. *Railroads and Rivers*. Boston: L. C. Page & Company, 1939.

Corliss, Carlton J. *Trails to Rails*. Chicago: Illinois Central System, 1934.

Crum, Josie Moore. *Rails Among the Peaks, Three Little Lines*. St. Paul, Minnesota: Railroader Printing House, 1956.

Dodge, Grenville M. *How We Built the Union Pacific Railway*. Washington, D. C.: The U. S. Government Printing Office, 1910.

Farrington, S. Kip, Jr. *Railroads of the Hour*. New York: Coward-McCann, Inc., 1958.

Greeley, Horace. *The American Conflict*. Hartford: O. D. Case & Co., 1866.

Hacker, Louis M., and Kendrick, Benjamin B. *The United States Since 1865*. New York: F. S. Crofts & Co., 1932.

Heath, Erle. *Seventy-five Years of Progress*. San Francisco: Southern Pacific Bureau of News, 1945.

Henry, Robert Selph. *This Fascinating Railroad Business*. New York: Bobbs-Merrill Co., 1942.

Herr, Kincaid. *The Louisville and Nashville Railroad*. Louisville, Kentucky: L & N Magazine, 1943.

Hill, James J. *Highways of Progress*. New York: Doubleday, Page 1910.

BIBLIOGRAPHY

Holbrook, Stewart H. *James J. Hill's Great Adventure*. New York: Railroad Magazine, February, 1955.
Holbrook, Stewart H. *Let Them Live*. New York: Macmillan Co., 1938.
Holbrook. *The Story of American Railroads*. New York: Crown Publishers, 1947.
Husband, Joseph. *The Story of the Pullman Car*. Chicago: A. C. McClurg & Company, 1917.
Jackson, Clarence S. *Picture Maker of the Old West*. New York: Charles Scribner's Sons, 1947.
Kennan, George. *E. H. Harriman, a Biography*. Boston: Houghton, Mifflin & Company, 1922.
Lee, Fred J. *Casey Jones*. Kingsport, Ten-

nessee: Southern Publishers, Inc., 1939.
Nevins, F. J. *Seventy Years of Service*. Chicago: Rock Island Lines, 1922.
One Hundred Years of Transportation Progress. The Pennsylvania Railroad Company, 1945.
Overton, R. C. *The First Ninety Years, An Historical Sketch of the Burlington Railroad*. Chicago: Burlington & Quincy Railroad, 1940.
The Railroad. The Atchison, Topeka and Santa Fe Railway Company, 1945.
The Railway Mail Association and the Railway Postal Clerk. Washington, D. C.: The Railway Mail Association, 1946.
Spearman, Frank H. *The Strategy of Great Railroads*. New York: Scribner's, 1904.

Thompson, Slason. *Short History of American Railways*. New York: D. Appleton & Company, 1925.
Union Pacific Railroad—A Brief History. Omaha: Department of Public Relations, Union Pacific Railroad.
Woodruff, Robert E. *Erie Railroad—Its Beginnings! 1851*. New York: The Newcomen Society, 1945.
The Young Folks Treasury. New York: The University Society, Inc., 1921.
Yungmeyer, D. W. *An Excursion into the Early History of the Chicago and Alton Railroad*. Springfield, Illinois: Journal of the Illinois State Historical Society, March, 1945.

FOR FURTHER READING

Young readers seeking further information on railroads in the days of steam will find the following books to be both helpful and entertaining:
Hubbard, Freeman H. *Round House Cat and Other Railroad Animals*. New York: Whittlesey House, McGraw-Hill, 1951.
Hubbard. *The Train That Never Came Back and Other Railroad Stories*. New York: Whittlesey House, McGraw-Hill, 1952.
McBride, Henry A. *Trains Rolling*. New York: Macmillan Co., 1953.

Morgan, David. *True Adventures of Railroaders*. Boston: Little Brown & Co., 1954.
Nathan, Adele. *The Building of the First Transcontinental Railroad*. New York: Random House, 1950.
Sagle, Lawrence W. *What Makes the Locomotive Go*. Ramsey, New Jersey: Model Craftsman Pub. Corp., 1945.
Shapiro, Irwin. *Casey Jones and Locomotive No. 638*. New York: Juilian Messner, Inc., 1944.

INDEX
Bold face indicates pages on which illustrations appear

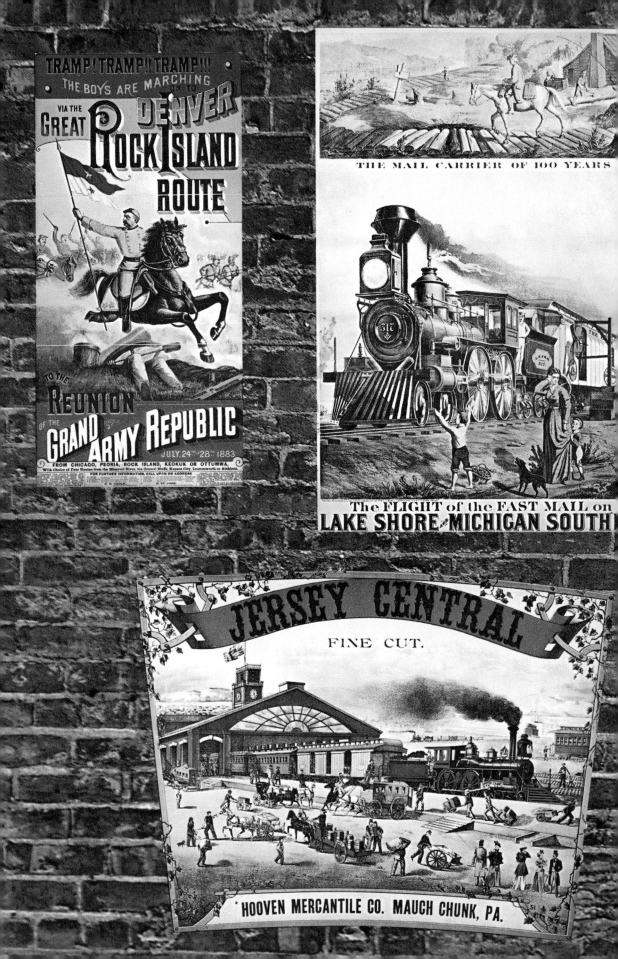